EXCEL outside the box

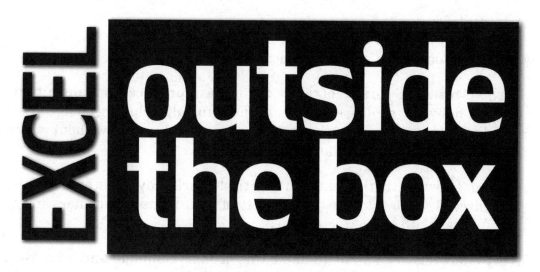

by Excel MVP
Bob Umlas

Holy Macro! Books
PO Box 82, Uniontown, OH 44685

Excel Outside the Box

Printed in USA by Malloy

First Printing: January 2012

Author: Bob Umlas

Technical Editor: Joseph Sorrenti

Copy Editor: Tyler Nash

Layout: Nellie J. Liwam

Cover Design: Shannon Mattiza, 6Ft4 Productions

Publisher: Bill Jelen

Indexer: Samuel T. Sharkowski

Published by: Holy Macro! Books, PO Box 82, Uniontown OH 44685

Distributed by Independent Publishers Group, Chicago IL

ISBN 978-1-61547-010-5 print, 978-1-61547-203-1 PDF

Library of Congress Control Number: 2011937995

Table of Contents

About the Author

Bob Umlas works for a major tax and accounting firm, using Microsoft Excel® eight hours a day, writing custom applications for staff and clients.

He has been using Excel since version 0.99 (on the Macintosh)! He was a contributing editor to Inside Microsoft Excel for many years, a magazine devoted exclusively to Microsoft Excel and published by The Cobb Group and later Ziff-Davis. At the time, most issues contained either an article by Mr. Umlas on using VBA (Visual Basic for Applications) or some tip or technique from him on using Excel. He has had more than 300 articles published on subjects ranging from beginner to advanced macros, and on tips, shortcuts, and general techniques using virtually every aspect of Excel.

Mr. Umlas was voted an "MVP" (Most Valuable Professional) by Microsoft each year since 1995 for his contributions to the various online Forums about Excel, and is known world-wide for his contributions in Excel. As an MVP, he meets yearly with his fellow-MVPs at Microsoft's headquarters in Redmond, WA, where he has access to the product developers. He has been a beta tester for new versions of Excel since version 1.5, and was asked by Microsoft for his input for newer versions of Excel. In 1995 he led a session called "Maximizing Excel Development Using Array Formulas" at Microsoft's Tech Ed Conference in New Orleans, and he led a session called Tips and Tricks at a Microsoft convention in New York City. He has also led two Excel sessions (Array Formulas, Tips & Tricks) at the Advisor's Developer Conference in San Francisco in February 1998.

Most recently, he led five sessions at an Excel User Conference in Atlantic City on Tips & Tricks, Array formulas, VBA, Formulas, and Userforms. He has led about seven or eight of these user conferences since 2005.

He is also the author of "This isn't Excel, it's Magic!" which is available from http://www.iil.com/publishing as well as from Amazon.com. (There are two versions of this book: One for Excel 2003, and one for Excel 2007).

He has co-authored several chapters in many books on Excel and has done the technical editing for six new books for Excel 2010 and has a white paper on array formulas published at http://www.emailoffice.com/excel/arrays-bobumlas.html .

Mr. Umlas used to co-lead the New York PC User's group on Excel every month for about 10 years. He has been teaching Excel to individuals and corporations for several years. Currently, Mr. Umlas leads a 12-hour class in Excel called Excel in Depth and a 6-hour class on VBA(see http://www.iil.com, click on "Virtual Classroom",then click on Virtual Classroom Schedule, choose Microsoft® Excel in Depths, click "See your selection", click "Course Outline").

Comments from readers:

"This book from the Excels Guru's Guru Bob Umlas will satisfy the Excel superstar in every office. Master tricks that mortals would think are impossible with Excel. The formulas in this book will solve every bizarre Excel problem."   – Bill Jelen, MrExcel. com, Excel MVP

"The hidden power of Excel with excellent examples, expertly explained by Bob Umlas" – Roger Govier, Excel MVP

"A book full of ingenuity" – Bill Manville, Excel MVP

"Seemingly impossible Excel challenges made simple! Another excellent book for the intermediate to advanced Excel addict, by Excel emperor Bob Umlas" – Jan Karel Pieterse, Excel MVP

Acknowledgments

I want to thank my fellow Excel MVP folks who were kind enough to read through this manuscript and make corrections, suggestions, etc. So thanks to Dick Kusleika, Jon Peltier, Richard Schollar, Ron de Bruin, Rick Rothstein, Jan Karel Pieterse, Roger Govier, Niek Otten, Bill Manville, Greg Truby, and especially Bill Jelen. I also want to thank my "official" technical editor and coworker, Joseph Sorrenti for his willingness to read through all the material and make suggestions for improvements and additions, as well as finding some typos!

I want to thank my wife for all her support of my taking the time (*our* time) to write this book as well as her unending love. She's an author herself (The Power of Acknowledgment), so she knows what goes into the creation of a book.

I also want to thank the Microsoft MVP program without which I would not have met such knowledgeable others to give a "second look" at the materials presented here.

Dedication

I want to dedicate the book to my family (wife Judy, son Jared, daughter Stefanie, son-in-law Shaun, granddaughter Lilith) and also to my fellow MVPs.

INTRODUCTION

There are many Excel books out there, why did I write this one? My daily work involves writing custom applications using Excel, and there are many problems I've had to think through to come up with a solution in Excel. I've used these solutions many times in my applications. I have not found any books or articles which described similar issues and solutions, yet it is hard to imagine that Excel developers in other companies hadn't also come up against these issues. So, given the feedback from my previous book ("This isn't Excel, it's Magic"), I thought it was time for another book to help the already-advanced Excel developer get past these hurdles.

So many times I've seen a data validation list contain many blanks at the bottom of the list (which was fixed in Excel 2010!), or with gaps, like this:

when it should look like this:

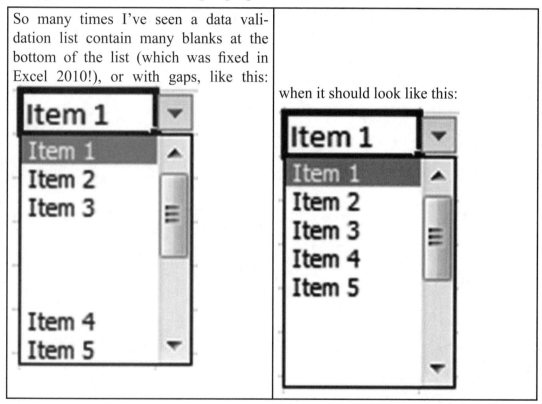

Even if the source contains those gaps. I describe how to fix that (and so many more things) in this book.

I show a lot of involved formulas but I decipher them step by step so they're no longer so formidable, like this array-entered one, for example:

=INDEX(A:A,SMALL(IF(ISNA(MATCH($A$1:$A$12,$C$1:$C$9,0)),ROW($1:$12),""),ROW(A2)))

This book is aimed at the company's already-expert Exceller, elevating him/her to the next level.

–Bob Umlas

CHAPTER 1 - TECHNIQUES

1-A Dilemma with Relative References

Figure 1 and Figure 2 show a simple worksheet normally and with formulas showing:

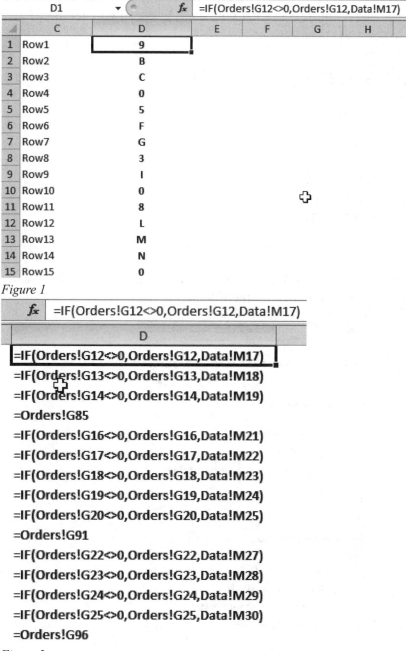

	D1			*fx*	=IF(Orders!G12<>0,Orders!G12,Data!M17)		
	C		D	E	F	G	H
1	Row1		9				
2	Row2		B				
3	Row3		C				
4	Row4		0				
5	Row5		5				
6	Row6		F				
7	Row7		G				
8	Row8		3				
9	Row9		I				
10	Row10		0				
11	Row11		8				
12	Row12		L				
13	Row13		M				
14	Row14		N				
15	Row15		0				

Figure 1

fx	=IF(Orders!G12<>0,Orders!G12,Data!M17)
	D
=IF(Orders!G12<>0,Orders!G12,Data!M17)
=IF(Orders!G13<>0,Orders!G13,Data!M18)
=IF(Orders!G14<>0,Orders!G14,Data!M19)
=Orders!G85
=IF(Orders!G16<>0,Orders!G16,Data!M21)
=IF(Orders!G17<>0,Orders!G17,Data!M22)
=IF(Orders!G18<>0,Orders!G18,Data!M23)
=IF(Orders!G19<>0,Orders!G19,Data!M24)
=IF(Orders!G20<>0,Orders!G20,Data!M25)
=Orders!G91
=IF(Orders!G22<>0,Orders!G22,Data!M27)
=IF(Orders!G23<>0,Orders!G23,Data!M28)
=IF(Orders!G24<>0,Orders!G24,Data!M29)
=IF(Orders!G25<>0,Orders!G25,Data!M30)
=Orders!G96

Figure 2

Assume this goes on for hundreds of rows.

Also assume you discovered that most of the formulas are wrong – you *really* wanted those cells which refer to Data to be 3 rows down. That is, in cell D1 you wanted the reference to be to cell M20, not M17. How can you fix it? There's nothing to replace – replacing 17 with 20 certainly won't help. You can't fix the first one and fill down because of the cells which are not of a like formula – for example, filling down would destroy the formula in cell D4. Figure 3 is what you want, how can you get there?

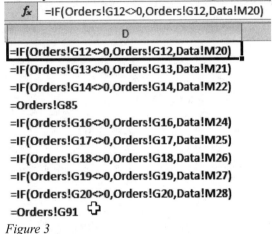

Figure 3

The answer (well, *one* answer, anyway) is to switch to R1C1 format. Yes, it actually *does* have a really good use! It's done here in the File menu, Options.

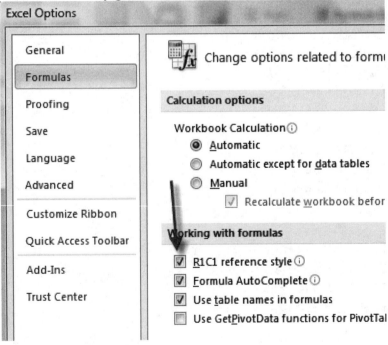

Figure 4

How does that help? Look at the underlying formulas here:

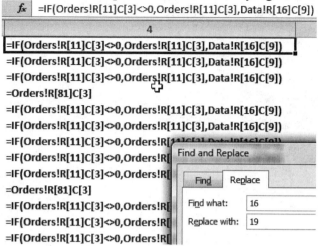

Figure 5

See those [16]'s? All you need to do is change them to [19]'s, with the result shown below:

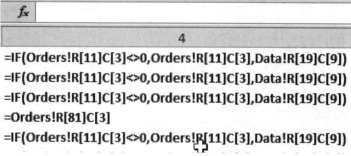

Figure 6

When you switch back to A1 notation (uncheck R1C1) you have this:

D
=IF(Orders!G12<>0,Orders!G12,Data!M20)
=IF(Orders!G13<>0,Orders!G13,Data!M21)
=IF(Orders!G14<>0,Orders!G14,Data!M22)
=Orders!G85
=IF(Orders!G16<>0,Orders!G16,Data!M24)
=IF(Orders!G17<>0,Orders!G17,Data!M25)
=IF(Orders!G18<>0,Orders!G18,Data!M26)
=IF(Orders!G19<>0,Orders!G19,Data!M27)
=IF(Orders!G20<>0,Orders!G20,Data!M28)
=Orders!G91

Figure 7

And you're done! But wait – here's an entirely different approach which also works well. First, create a new sheet, say that's Sheet4. It will remain empty for this process, but will serve an important function as you will soon see. Change the above formulas by changing the reference from Data to Sheet4, as seen here:

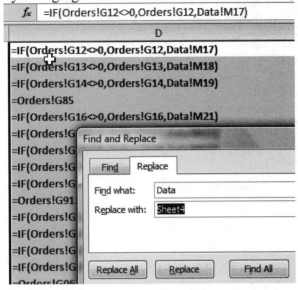

Figure 8

And afterwards as you see here:

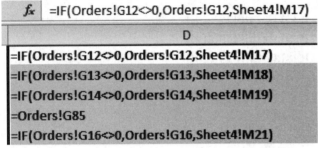

Figure 9

Now go to Sheet4, select cells M1:M3, Insert cells (Home tab), shifting down:

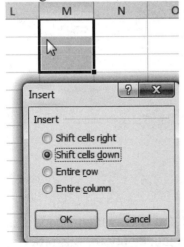

Figure 10

Return to the main sheet and look at the formulas:

| *fx* | =IF(Orders!G12<>0,Orders!G12,Sheet4!M20) |

D
=IF(Orders!G12<>0,Orders!G12,Sheet4!M20)
=IF(Orders!G13<>0,Orders!G13,Sheet4!M21)
=IF(Orders!G14<>0,Orders!G14,Sheet4!M22)
=Orders!G85
=IF(Orders!G16<>0,Orders!G16,Sheet4!M24)
=IF(Orders!G17<>0,Orders!G17,Sheet4!M25)
=IF(Orders!G18<>0,Orders!G18,Sheet4!M26)
=IF(Orders!G19<>0,Orders!G19,Sheet4!M27)
=IF(Orders!G20<>0,Orders!G20,Sheet4!M28)

Figure 11

Now change Sheet4 back to Data and you're done:

| *fx* | =IF(Orders!G12<>0,Orders!G12,Data!M20) |

D	E	F
9		
B		
C		

Figure 12

2-Build a Formula with a Formula

Look at the worksheet in Figure 13 on the next page.

You can see that some information from Sheet2 is being picked up on Sheet1 via an INDIRECT formula. A quick look at Sheet2 (nothing special) in Figure 14.

Why use INDIRECT? Perhaps the information on Sheet2 may be cut/pasted elsewhere, but you are interested in the data in A1:A22, regardless of how information may be moved around.

What's the issue? Look at the formulas in Sheet1 in Figure 15.

The problem is, how can you create these formulas without typing each one (or without reverting to creating a VBA procedure!)? You can't fill the formula down from A1, because it's all text, and the formula will stay the same. The answer lies in *building the formula* with a formula. Let's see what this means (Figure 16).

Notice that the formulas in column A *seem* to be the same as the previous screenshot, but look at what's in the formula bar! You are looking at ="=INDIRECT(""Sheet2!A" &ROW(A1)&""")" which is the formula you *want* to be in cell A1, but entirely built as a string except the reference to ROW(A1) to give us the one you want.

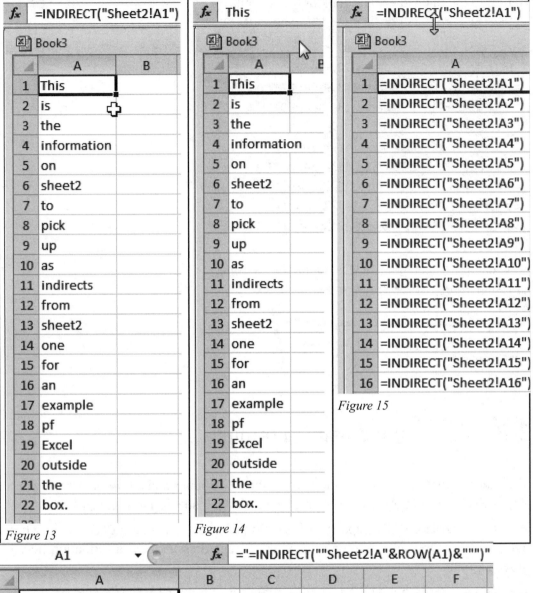

fx	=INDIRECT("Sheet2!A1")

Book3

	A	B
1	This	
2	is	
3	the	
4	information	
5	on	
6	sheet2	
7	to	
8	pick	
9	up	
10	as	
11	indirects	
12	from	
13	sheet2	
14	one	
15	for	
16	an	
17	example	
18	pf	
19	Excel	
20	outside	
21	the	
22	box.	

Figure 13

fx	This

Book3

	A	B
1	This	
2	is	
3	the	
4	information	
5	on	
6	sheet2	
7	to	
8	pick	
9	up	
10	as	
11	indirects	
12	from	
13	sheet2	
14	one	
15	for	
16	an	
17	example	
18	pf	
19	Excel	
20	outside	
21	the	
22	box.	

Figure 14

fx	=INDIRECT("Sheet2!A1")

Book3

	A
1	=INDIRECT("Sheet2!A1")
2	=INDIRECT("Sheet2!A2")
3	=INDIRECT("Sheet2!A3")
4	=INDIRECT("Sheet2!A4")
5	=INDIRECT("Sheet2!A5")
6	=INDIRECT("Sheet2!A6")
7	=INDIRECT("Sheet2!A7")
8	=INDIRECT("Sheet2!A8")
9	=INDIRECT("Sheet2!A9")
10	=INDIRECT("Sheet2!A10")
11	=INDIRECT("Sheet2!A11")
12	=INDIRECT("Sheet2!A12")
13	=INDIRECT("Sheet2!A13")
14	=INDIRECT("Sheet2!A14")
15	=INDIRECT("Sheet2!A15")
16	=INDIRECT("Sheet2!A16")

Figure 15

A1	▼	*fx*	="=INDIRECT(""Sheet2!A"&ROW(A1)&""")"

	A	B	C	D	E	F
1	=INDIRECT("Sheet2!A1")					
2	=INDIRECT("Sheet2!A2")					
3	=INDIRECT("Sheet2!A3")					
4	=INDIRECT("Sheet2!A4")					
5	=INDIRECT("Sheet2!A5")					
6	=INDIRECT("Sheet2!A6")					

Figure 16

fx ="=INDIRECT(""Sheet2!A"&ROW(A1)&""")"

Figure 17

becomes

fx ="=INDIRECT(""Sheet2!A"&{1}&""")"

Figure 18

and then

fx ="=INDIRECT(""Sheet2!A"&{1}&""")"

Figure 19

becomes

fx ="=INDIRECT("{"Sheet2!A1"}")"

Figure 20

This becomes what you see in cell A1. Now when this formula is filled down, the ROW(A1) becomes ROW(A2), etc. and you have what you need. However, this is not ready for use – it's not an INDIRECT formula, it's a text string *containing* the word INDIRECT, etc. What's left to do is copy/paste special values. I like doing it this way especially since after the fill down, my hand is on the mouse.

Right-click the *border* of the selection and drag away (anywhere), and then drag the selection right back to where it started. This is what you see when you right-click drag the border away without letting go of the mouse:

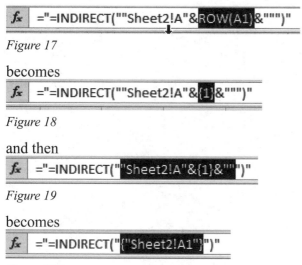

	A	B	C
1	=INDIRECT("Sheet2!A1")		
2	=INDIRECT("Sheet2!A2")		
3	=INDIRECT("Sheet2!A3")		
4	=INDIRECT("Sheet2!A4")		
5	=INDIRECT("Sheet2!A5")		
6	=INDIRECT("Sheet2!A6")		
7	=INDIRECT("Sheet2!A7")		B1:B22
8	=INDIRECT("Sheet2!A8")		

Figure 21

When you drag back, before letting go you see Figure 22:

A1		*fx*	=
	A	**B**	
1	=INDIRECT("Sheet2!A1")		
2	=INDIRECT("Sheet2!A2")		
3	=INDIRECT("Sheet2!A3")		
4	=INDIRECT("Sheet2!A4")		
5	=INDIRECT("Sheet2!A5")		
6	=INDIRECT("Sheet2!A6")		
7	=INDIRECT("Sheet2!A7")	A1:A22	
8	=INDIRECT("Sheet2!A8")		
9	=INDIRECT("Sheet2!A9")		

Figure 22

When you let go you'll see this:

4	=INDIRECT("Sheet2!A4")		
5	=INDIRECT("Sheet2!A5")		
6	=INDIRECT("Sheet2!A6")		
7	=INDIRECT("Sheet2!A7")		
8	=INDIRECT("Sheet2!A8")		
9	=INDIRECT("Sheet2!A9")		
10	=INDIRECT("Sheet2!A	**Move Here**	
11	=INDIRECT("Sheet2!A	**Copy Here**	
12	=INDIRECT("Sheet2!A	Copy Here as Values Only	
13	=INDIRECT("Sheet2!A	Copy Here as Formats Only	
14	=INDIRECT("Sheet2!A	Link Here	
15	=INDIRECT("Sheet2!A	Create Hyperlink Here	

Figure 23

And the highlighted option is the feature you use to get this:

A1		*fx*	=INDIRECT("Sheet2!A1")		
	↓ **A**	**B**	**C**	**D**	
1	=INDIRECT("Sheet2!A1")				
2	=INDIRECT("Sheet2!A2")				
3	=INDIRECT("Sheet2!A3")				
4	=INDIRECT("Sheet2!A4")				
5	=INDIRECT("Sheet2!A5")				
6	=INDIRECT("Sheet2!A6")				
7	=INDIRECT("Sheet2!A7")				
8	=INDIRECT("Sheet2!A8")				

Figure 24

It doesn't look like anything changed, but look at the formula bar – it's no longer a text string. However, the formulas in column A need to be coerced into formulas. This can be easily done by replacing "=" with "=". Replacing "=" with "=" doesn't seem like it would accomplish much, but in fact, it will force Excel to reevaluate each cell and realize that it's a formula.

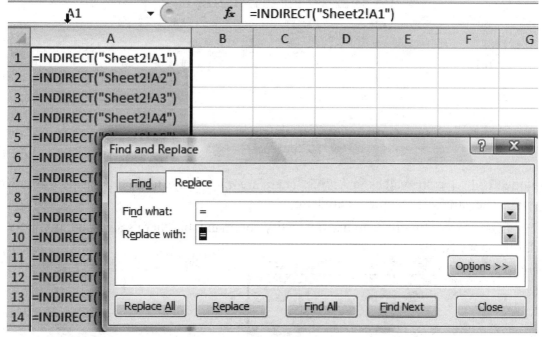

Figure 25

You will get this:

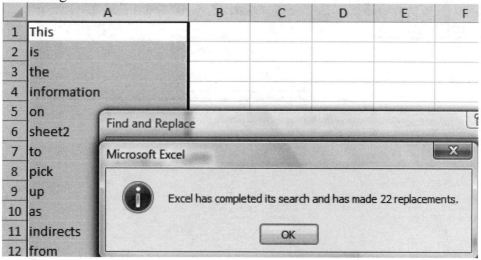

Figure 26

3-Combining a List of Values into One

A reader recently posted a question about the following. He wanted to take the numbers in column A, below, and put them in one cell, separated by commas:

A	B	C
123456		123456, 33, 827382, 91872, 1241, 3312, 18
33		
827382		
91872		
1241		
3312		
18		

Figure 27

Notice cell C1 is the values in A1:A7. There are a few ways to do this (aside from re-typing the values!!) Examine them here.

The first approach might be to use the justify command, but there's a gotcha. If you try it, this happens:

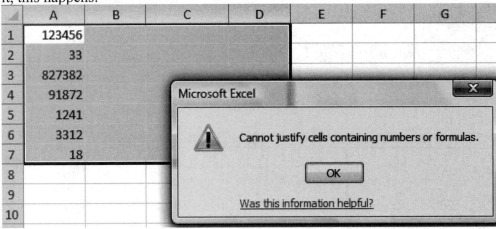

Figure 28

One way to solve it is this:

B1				f_x	=A1&","

	A	B	C	D
1	123456	123456,		
2	33	33,		
3	827382	827382,		
4	91872	91872,		
5	1241	1241,		
6	3312	3312,		
7	18	18,		

Figure 29

Notice that the formulas in column B simply append a comma to column A. You don't want the last one (cell B7) to contain a comma, so you change that one's formula:

B7				f_x	=A7&""

	A	B	C	D
1	123456	123456,		
2	33	33,		
3	827382	827382,		
4	91872	91872,		
5	1241	1241,		
6	3312	3312,		
7	18	18		

Figure 30

Instead of using just =A7, you still append the "" which is a null string but also is *text*, not a number. If you read the previous alert message, you see that you can't use Justify on numbers. OK, now copy/paste special values in column B:

Make this selection (arbitrarily wide to accommodate all the values):

				f_x	=A1&","

B	C	D	E	F
123456,				
33,				
827382,				
91872,				
1241,				
3312,				
18				

Figure 31

and the Justify command does the job, seen in Figure 32:

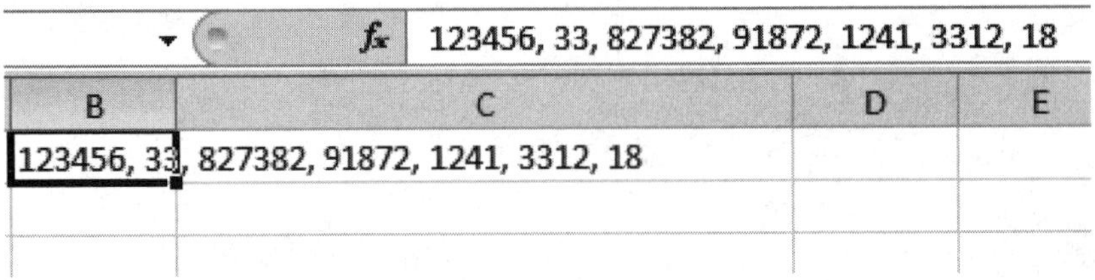

	B	C	D	E
fx	123456, 33, 827382, 91872, 1241, 3312, 18			
	123456, 33, 827382, 91872, 1241, 3312, 18			

Figure 32

OK, I mentioned other ways. Here's one. Look at the formula in B2:

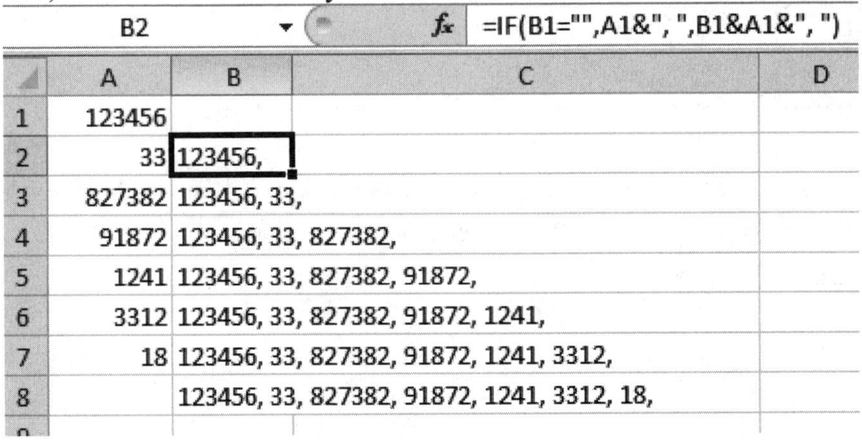

B2 fx =IF(B1="",A1&", ",B1&A1&", ")

	A	B	C	D
1	123456			
2	33	123456,		
3	827382	123456, 33,		
4	91872	123456, 33, 827382,		
5	1241	123456, 33, 827382, 91872,		
6	3312	123456, 33, 827382, 91872, 1241,		
7	18	123456, 33, 827382, 91872, 1241, 3312,		
8		123456, 33, 827382, 91872, 1241, 3312, 18,		

Figure 33

Start in B2 because the cell above needs to be referenced to see if it is empty. If the cell above is empty, use A1 and append a comma, otherwise take the cell above and append it to the cell to the left. As you can see, it grows as you fill down. The formula in B3 is =IF(B2="",A2&", ",B2&A2&", "). So the answer is in cell B8 – all you need do is copy/paste values for B8 and chop off the trailing comma.

4-Comparing Worksheets

Suppose you need to see if 2 worksheets are identical. You may try to do this visually or maybe even use VBA to find the differences, but let's see if there's an easy way. Look at these 2 sheets from the same workbook:

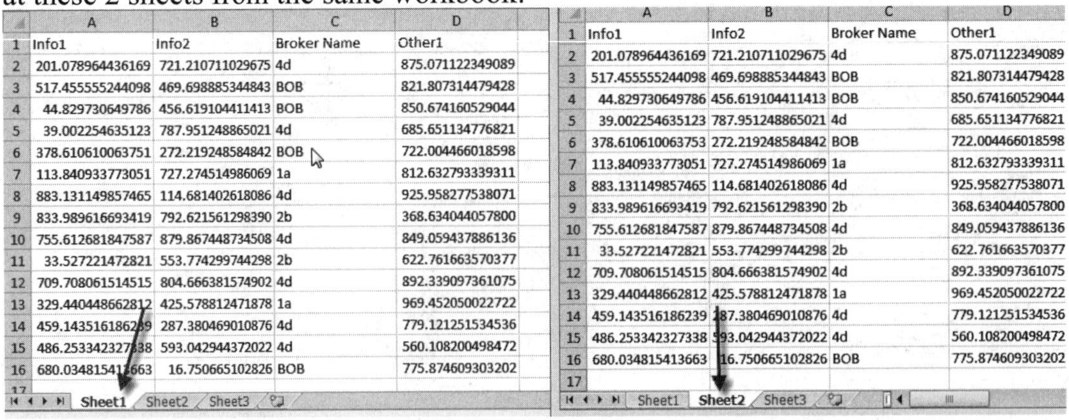

Sheet1

	A	B	C	D
1	Info1	Info2	Broker Name	Other1
2	201.078964436169	721.210711029675	4d	875.071122349089
3	517.455555244098	469.698885344843	BOB	821.807314479428
4	44.829730649786	456.619104411413	BOB	850.674160529044
5	39.002254635123	787.951248865021	4d	685.651134776821
6	378.610610063751	272.219248584842	BOB	722.004466018598
7	113.840933773051	727.274514986069	1a	812.632793339311
8	883.131149857465	114.681402618086	4d	925.958277538071
9	833.989616693419	792.621561298390	2b	368.634044057800
10	755.612681847587	879.867448734508	4d	849.059437886136
11	33.527221472821	553.774299744298	2b	622.761663570377
12	709.708061514515	804.666381574902	4d	892.339097361075
13	329.440448662812	425.578812471878	1a	969.452050022722
14	459.143516186239	287.380469010876	4d	779.121251534536
15	486.253342327338	593.042944372022	4d	560.108200498472
16	680.034815413663	16.750665102826	BOB	775.874609303202
17				

Sheet2

	A	B	C	D
1	Info1	Info2	Broker Name	Other1
2	201.078964436169	721.210711029675	4d	875.071122349089
3	517.455555244098	469.698885344843	BOB	821.807314479428
4	44.829730649786	456.619104411413	BOB	850.674160529044
5	39.002254635123	787.951248865021	4d	685.651134776821
6	378.610610063753	272.219248584842	BOB	722.004466018598
7	113.840933773051	727.274514986069	1a	812.632793339311
8	883.131149857465	114.681402618086	4d	925.958277538071
9	833.989616693419	792.621561298390	2b	368.634044057800
10	755.612681847587	879.867448734508	4d	849.059437886136
11	33.527221472821	553.774299744298	2b	622.761663570377
12	709.708061514515	804.666381574902	4d	892.339097361075
13	329.440448662812	425.578812471878	1a	969.452050022722
14	459.143516186239	287.380469010876	4d	779.121251534536
15	486.253342327338	593.042944372022	4d	560.108200498472
16	680.034815413663	16.750665102826	BOB	775.874609303202
17				

Figure 34

Notice that when looking at Sheet1 and Sheet2, they certainly *look* the same, but there are differences. A pretty simple way to see the differences is by using a third worksheet (or even another workbook), and entering this simple formula:

A1	▾		f_x	=IF(Sheet1!A1=Sheet2!A1,"","•")		
	A	B	C	D	E	F	G
1							

Figure 35

It's comparing cell A1 (as a relative reference) in Sheet1 to Sheet2, and when there's a difference, it puts in a bullet (Alt+7 (7 from the numeric keypad)). So, looking at this, you can see where there are differences:

A1	▾		f_x	=IF(Sheet1!A1=Sheet2!A1,"","•")		
	A	B	C	D	E	F	G
1							
2							
3			•				
4							
5							
6	•						

Figure 36

Cell C3 looks the same in both sheets, but on further examination you could determine that there's a trailing space in one and not in the other. Cell A5 ends in 751 on Sheet1 and 753 on Sheet2.

If you wanted to compare not just values but differences in formulas, you would have to make a change first. A formula such as =1+3 would be treated the same as =2+2 since Excel is comparing the results. You would need to do a global replace of "=" with "x=", changing all formulas to text, then the comparison sheet would show any differences.

Once found and corrected, you could then change "x=" to "=".

5-Creating a Series of the 15th of the Month and the Last Day of the Month

It's not *too* difficult to create Figure 37 without using formulas.

How would you go about doing it? You can't use any series, because if you tried by starting to use Figure 38, and drag the Fill Handle, you'd see this mess in Figure 39 and so on:

	A
1	1/15/2011
2	1/31/2011
3	2/15/2011
4	2/28/2011
5	3/15/2011
6	3/31/2011
7	4/15/2011
8	4/30/2011
9	5/15/2011
10	5/31/2011
11	6/15/2011
12	6/30/2011
13	7/15/2011
14	7/31/2011
15	8/15/2011
16	8/31/2011
17	9/15/2011
18	9/30/2011
19	10/15/2011
20	10/31/2011
21	11/15/2011
22	11/30/2011
23	12/15/2011
24	12/31/2011

Figure 37

A1

	A
1	1/15/2011
2	1/31/2011
3	
4	
5	
6	

Figure 38

	A
1	1/15/2011
2	1/31/2011
3	2/16/2011
4	3/4/2011
5	3/20/2011
6	4/5/2011
7	4/21/2011
8	5/7/2011
9	5/23/2011
10	6/8/2011

Figure 39

Here are two approaches: First, enter 1/15/11. Select the date and the following blank cell as shown in Figure 40. *Right-mouse* drag the Fill Handle. When you let go of the right mouse button, you'll see Figure 41, and when you select Fill Months, you'll get Figure 42:

	A
1	1/15/2011
2	
3	
4	
5	
6	
7	
8	
9	
10	
11	
12	
13	
14	
15	
16	
17	
18	
19	
20	
21	
22	
23	

Figure 40

	A	B	C	D
1	1/15/2011			
2				
3				
4				
5				
6				
7				
8				
9				
10				
11				
12		Copy Cells		
13				
14		Fill _S_eries		
15		Fill _F_ormatting Only		
16		Fill With_o_ut Formatting		
17		Fill _D_ays		
18		Fill _W_eekdays		
19		Fill _M_onths		
20		Fill _Y_ears		
21		Linear Trend		

Figure 41

	A
1	1/15/2011
2	
3	2/15/2011
4	
5	3/15/2011
6	
7	4/15/2011
8	
9	5/15/2011
10	
11	6/15/2011
12	
13	7/15/2011
14	
15	8/15/2011
16	
17	9/15/2011
18	
19	10/15/2011
20	
21	11/15/2011
22	
23	12/15/2011
24	

Figure 42

Now, you can Go To Special (on the home tab, or press F5, click Special) – see Figure 43. Select blanks (Figure 44). And you will have Figure 45. Now, with cell A2 active, enter =A3-15 and instead of pressing Enter, press Ctrl+Enter to see Figure 46. You can manually enter 12/31/2011 in cell A24.

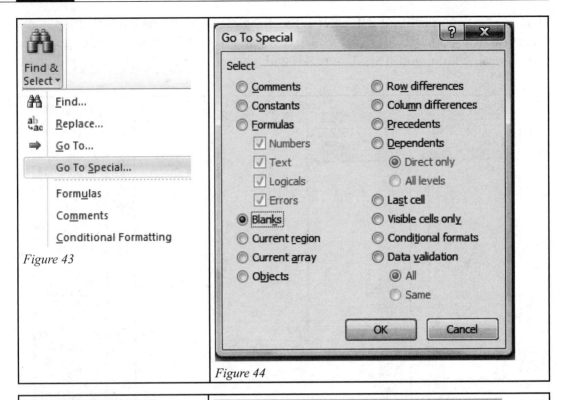

Figure 43

Figure 44

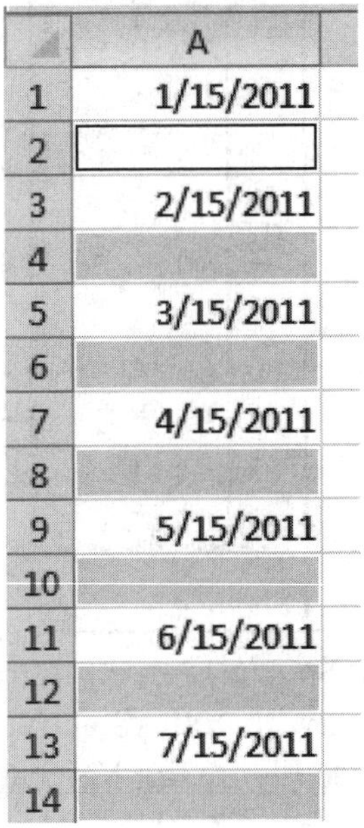

Figure 45

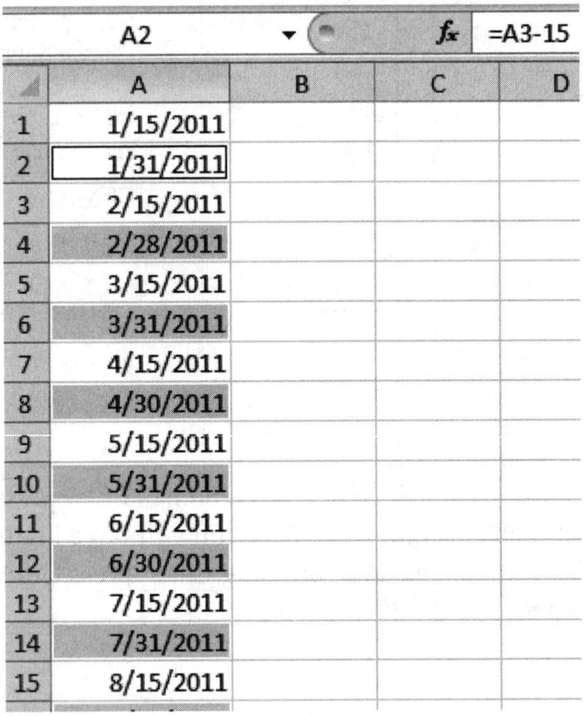

Figure 46

Here's a second approach: After having the 1/15/2011 in A1, and blank in A2, then 2/15/2011 in A3, etc., enter this in C1:

C
1/31/2011

Figure 47

Again use the right-click fill handle down to C24 and select months to generate the end of each month (Figure 48). Next, copy this range (C1:C24), click in cell A2 (not A1), and Paste Special. Be sure to include Skip Blanks (Figure 49):

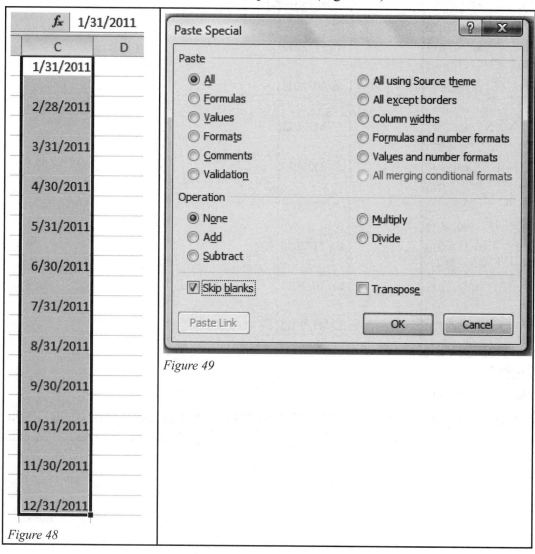

Figure 49

Figure 48

You will wind up with this:

	A	B	C	D
A2	▾	🔵	*fx*	1/31/2011
1	1/15/2011		1/31/2011	
2	1/31/2011			
3	2/15/2011		2/28/2011	
4	2/28/2011			
5	3/15/2011		3/31/2011	
6	3/31/2011			
7	4/15/2011		4/30/2011	
8	4/30/2011			
9	5/15/2011		5/31/2011	
10	5/31/2011			
11	6/15/2011		6/30/2011	
12	6/30/2011			
13	7/15/2011		7/31/2011	
14	7/31/2011			
15	8/15/2011		8/31/2011	
16	8/31/2011			
17	9/15/2011		9/30/2011	
18	9/30/2011			
19	10/15/2011		10/31/2011	
20	10/31/2011			
21	11/15/2011		11/30/2011	
22	11/30/2011			
23	12/15/2011		12/31/2011	
24	12/31/2011			

Figure 50

Now clear column C.

A third approach: Enter 1/15/2011 and 1/31/2011 in A1:A2. Select both cells. Right-drag the fill handle down to A24. When you release the fill handle, choose Fill Months from flyout menu that appears.

6-Match Colors

Suppose you inherit the worksheet shown here:

◢	A	B	C	D
1				
2				
3				
4				
5				
6				
7				
8				
9				

Figure 51

You want to make the FONT of column E equal to the color in A1:C7. How do you find the correct color? If you click on the *arrow* next to the Fill Color icon on the Home tab in the Font group, then click More Colors:

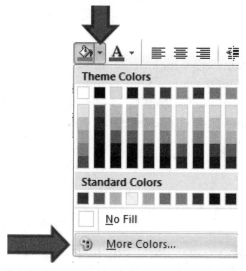

Figure 52

When you click on the "Custom" tab, you'll see Figure 53:

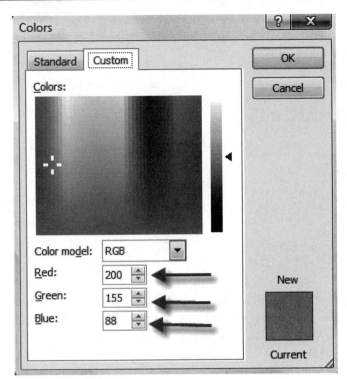

Figure 53

The RGB numbers (Red, Green, Blue) are the numbers which make up the color. You can now use these in the Font Color to make the font the same. Select column E, use the drop down arrow next to the Font Color icon, select the Custom tab and enter the same values Then once you type something into column E it will be the same color.

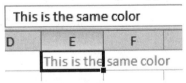

Figure 54

There is another way to do this using the VBE (Visual Basic Environment). Press Alt+F11, then Ctrl+G (to get the immediate window), and enter this code:

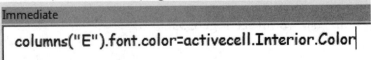

Figure 55

7-Reorganization of Data

Look at the spreadsheet:

▲	A	B
1	1	Name
2	1	Address
3	1	City
4	1	State
5	1	Zip
6	1	Telephone
7	1	Fax
8	1	Email
9	2	Bob Umlas
10	2	123 Main Street
11	2	MyCity
12	2	New York
13	2	01111
14	2	555-102-9382
15	2	555-102-9383
16	2	BobUmlas@BobUmlas.Com

Figure 56

Suppose this continues down hundreds of rows. Suppose you wanted the data to be rearranged so that it looks like this:

C	D	E	F	G	H	I	J	K
1	Name	Address	City	State	Zip	Telephone	Fax	Email
2	Bob Umlas	123 Main Street	MyCity	New York	01111	555-102-9382	555-102-9283	BobUmlas@BobUmlas.Com

Figure 57

As well as filled down.

The setup is not intuitive. You would like the formulas in C1:K2, above, to be:

C	D	E	F	G	H	I	J	K
=A1	=B1	=B2	=B3	=B4	=B5	=B6	=B7	=B8
=A9	=B9	=B10	=B11	=B12	=B13	=B14	=B15	=B16

Figure 58

If you set up the initial two rows like Figure 58 above and fill down, the result is what you see in Figure 59:

C	D	E	F	G	H	I	J	K
=A1	=B1	=B2	=B3	=B4	=B5	=B6	=B7	=B8
=A9	=B9	=B10	=B11	=B12	=B13	=B14	=B15	=B16
=A3	=B3	=B4	=B5	=B6	=B7	=B8	=B9	=B10
=A11	=B11	=B12	=B13	=B14	=B15	=B16	=B17	=B18
=A5	=B5	=B6	=B7	=B8	=B9	=B10	=B11	=B12

Figure 59

Which is definitely not going to work.

But if you set it up manually as shown here:

C	D
xa1	xb1
xa9	xb9

Figure 60

where you reference column A in column C (using x instead of "=", so this is all text), then select D1 and use the fill handle to drag to the right, you see this:

C	D	E	F	G	H	I	J	K
xa1	xb1							
xa9	xb9							

Figure 61

Which becomes this when you let go of the mouse:

C	D	E	F	G	H	I	J	K
xa1	xb1	xb2	xb3	xb4	xb5	xb6	xb7	xb8
xa9	xb9							

Figure 62

Repeat with D2:

C	D	E	F	G	H	I	J	K
xa1	xb1	xb2	xb3	xb4	xb5	xb6	xb7	xb8
xa9	xb9	xb10	xb11	xb12	xb13	xb14	xb15	xb16

Figure 63

Now select C1:K2 and use the fill handle to drag down and you will get this:

C	D	E	F	G	H	I	J	K
xa1	xb1	xb2	xb3	xb4	xb5	xb6	xb7	xb8
xa9	xb9	xb10	xb11	xb12	xb13	xb14	xb15	xb16
xa17	xb17	xb18	xb19	xb20	xb21	xb22	xb23	xb24
xa25	xb25	xb26	xb27	xb28	xb29	xb30	xb31	xb32
xa33	xb33	xb34	xb35	xb36	xb37	xb38	xb39	xb40

Figure 64

Lastly, replace "x" with "=":

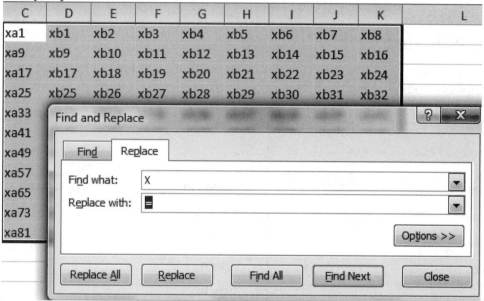

Figure 65

Resulting in this:

C	D	E	F	G	H	I	J	K
=A1	=B1	=B2	=B3	=B4	=B5	=B6	=B7	=B8
=A9	=B9	=B10	=B11	=B12	=B13	=B14	=B15	=B16
=A17	=B17	=B18	=B19	=B20	=B21	=B22	=B23	=B24
=A25	=B25	=B26	=B27	=B28	=B29	=B30	=B31	=B32
=A33	=B33	=B34	=B35	=B36	=B37	=B38	=B39	=B40
=A41	=B41	=B42	=B43	=B44	=B45	=B46	=B47	=B48
=A49	=B49	=B50	=B51	=B52	=B53	=B54	=B55	=B56
=A57	=B57	=B58	=B59	=B60	=B61	=B62	=B63	=B64
=A65	=B65	=B66	=B67	=B68	=B69	=B70	=B71	=B72
=A73	=B73	=B74	=B75	=B76	=B77	=B78	=B79	=B80
=A81	=B81	=B82	=B83	=B84	=B85	=B86	=B87	=B88

Figure 66

You now have the formula you want. You are seeing the formula because the worksheet is set to Show Formulas which is easily toggled by Ctrl+`. When you use the toggle again, and adjust the column widths, you see this:

C	D	E	F	G	H	I	J	K
1	Name	Address	City	State	Zip	Telephone	Fax	Email
2	Bob Umlas	123 Main Street	MyCity	New York	01111	555-102-9382	555-102-9383	BobUmlas@BobUmlas.Com
3	Name2	Address2	City2	State2	Zip2	Telephone2	Fax2	Email2
4	Name3	Address3	City3	State3	Zip3	Telephone3	Fax3	Email3
5	Name4	Address4	City4	State4	Zip4	Telephone4	Fax4	Email4
6	Name5	Address5	City5	State5	Zip5	Telephone5	Fax5	Email5

Figure 67

8-Scrolling Text

Since this is a book, I can't really show you what scrolling text looks like. Here are a few screenshots from pressing the button once. Look at Figure 68 through Figure 73:

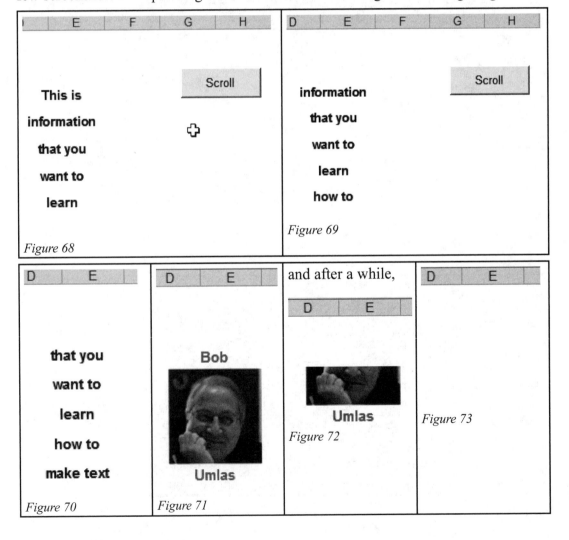

Figure 68

Figure 69

Figure 70

Figure 71

and after a while,

Figure 72

Figure 73

The meat of the text is kept outside anyone's view, as seen in Figure 74, and it continues to Figure 75:

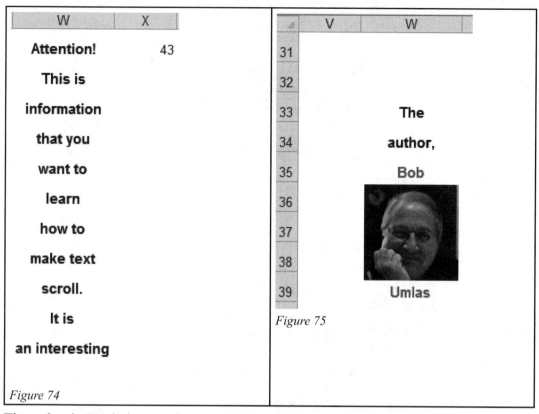

Figure 74

Figure 75

The value in X1 is key to the scrolling process. The first thing you need is to take a picture of some cells, using the camera tool. In order to make this work properly, it has to be put into the QAT. You'll need to do that first by following these steps: Right-click anywhere on the ribbon, and select "Customize Quick Access Toolbar…" and you'll see Figure 76 (showing the top left corner only):

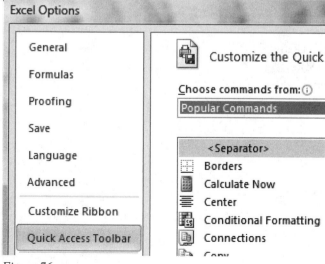

Figure 76

Change Popular Commands to "All Commands":

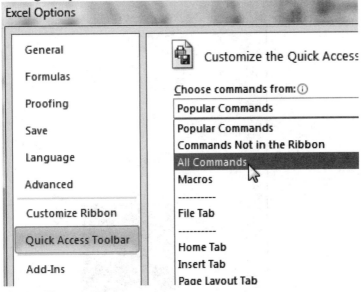

Figure 77

Scroll to Camera, and click Add:

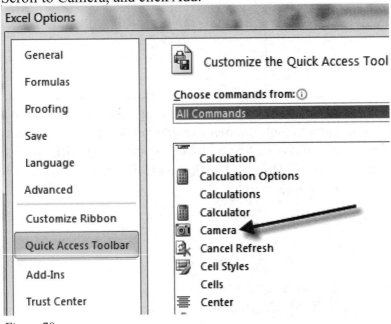

Figure 78

Select any cell, click the camera tool, then click where you want the scrolling to show, like near cell D1:

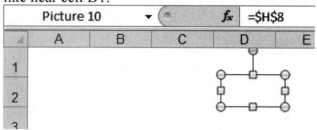

Figure 79

The formula bar shows H8 because that was the arbitrary cell you had selected when you clicked the tool. Next, you need to decide how many rows of data you want to show in the scrolling. Perhaps five, which you would set up in a defined name which you might call "Piece":

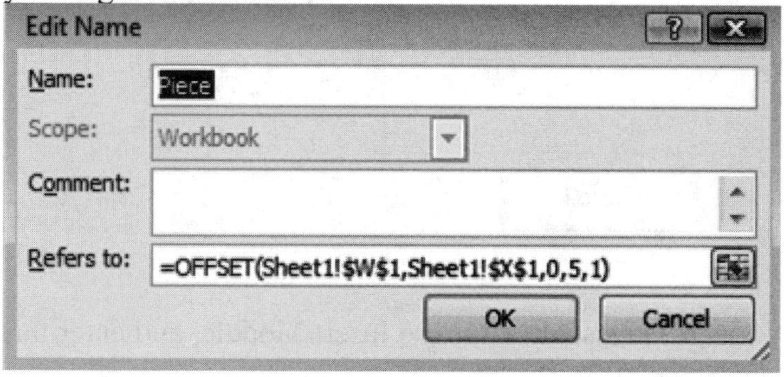

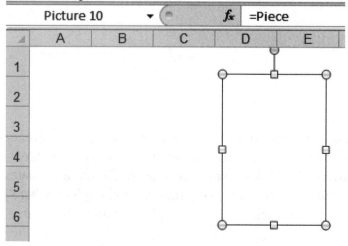

Figure 80

Notice that it's an offset of cell W1, where all the "real" text to scroll exists, and it's offset by whatever number is in cell X1. Then the shape is determined to be five rows by one column. When you next change the $H$8 in the formula bar to Piece, you see the new shape:

Figure 81

While its selected, press Ctrl+1 to bring up the Format dialog, and it will show no lines:

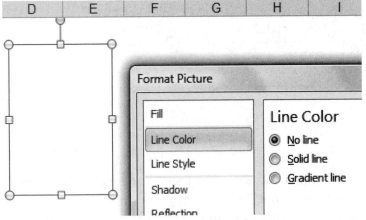

Figure 82

Now, when you click off of the picture, you will see nothing:

Scroll

Figure 83

Next, you need to look at the macro. Press Alt+F11, use Insert/Module, and enter this simple code:

```
(General)

Sub Scroller()
    For i = 0 To 43
        Range("X1").Value = i
        Calculate
        For j = 1 To 20000000: Next
    Next
End Sub
```

Figure 84

There's a loop in which the variable i goes from 0 to 43, because there are 39 rows of information in the text to scroll, and you want it to scroll beyond it, out of view. Computers are fast, so each time through the "i" loop you calculate (so the Offset updates and the new text shows up in the picture), and then a very tight do-nothing loop where j goes from 1 to 20,000,000! You can adjust this value for speed. The larger the number, the slower the scroll.

The colon separates the statement and acts like a new line. Figure 85 and Figure 86 are equivalent:

```
For j = 1 To 20000000: Next
```

Figure 85

```
For j = 1 To 20000000
Next
```

Figure 86

Lastly, you need to link the button to the code (see Figure 88 and Figure 89 to see how to put a Forms button on the sheet), which is done by right-clicking the button, selecting Assign Macro:

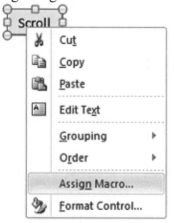

Figure 87

If the macro was written *before* creating the button, then as soon as the button is created you'd be presented with the form to link it to the macro as seen in Figure 88 and Figure 89:

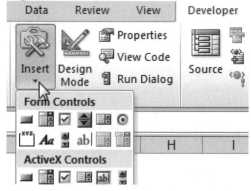

Figure 88

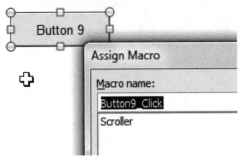

Figure 89

In case you don't see the Developer tab, you can have it show by right-clicking any part of the ribbon, select Customize the Ribbon:

Add to Quick Access Toolbar

Customize Quick Access Toolbar...

Show Quick Access Toolbar Below the Ribbon

Customize the Ribbon...

Minimize the Ribbon

Figure 90

Check the Developer checkbox:

Customize the Ribbon: ⓘ

Main Tabs

Main Tabs
- ☑ Home
- ☑ Insert
- ☑ Page Layout
- ☑ Formulas
- ☑ Data
- ☑ Review
- ☑ View
- ☑ Developer
  - Code
  - Add-Ins
  - Controls
  - XML
  - Modify
- ☑ Add-Ins
- ☑ Background Removal

Figure 91

If you are using Excel 2007, you will see the access to the Developer tab in the Office button, Excel Options, Popular category, Show Developer Tab In The Ribbon.

9-Sequences

Suppose you're keeping track of coin flipping and you want to gather some information on the longest sequence of heads; or how many times a sequence of 4 heads came up, etc. Figure 92 shows a sample worksheet:

A
1 T
2 H
3 H
4 H
5 H
6 H
7 H
8 T
9 H
10 H
11 T
12 H
13 H
14 H
15 H
16 T
17 H
18 H
19 H
20 T
21 T
22 H
23 T
24 T
25 T
26 H
27 H
28 H
29 T

Figure 92

One approach to start is to match "T" as an offset:

The formula

f_x =MATCH("t",OFFSET(A1,0,0,100,1),0)-1

Figure 93

in B1, filled down yields these numbers:

	A	B
1	T	0
2	H	6
3	H	5
4	H	4
5	H	3
6	H	2
7	H	1
8	T	0
9	H	2
10	H	1
11	T	0
12	H	4
13	H	3
14	H	2
15	H	1
16	T	0
17	H	3
18	H	2
19	H	1
20	T	0

Figure 94

It's an interesting start – the 6 in B2 shows a string of six heads, and the 2 in B9 shows a string of two heads, etc., but you need to distinguish the 2 in B6, B14, and B18 as not being significant or useful, since these are not the beginning values of the counts. The -1 at the end of the MATCH formula is needed to get a true count. Matching a "T" from cell B2 would find it in the seventh cell down, indicating 6 heads, hence you need to subtract 1. The 100 in the OFFSET function is an arbitrarily large enough number to ensure finding a "T" (there likely won't be 100 heads in a row!) – and you can change this to 1000.

So how can you get rid of the extraneous values? Look at this:

B2			f_x	=IF(A1="t",MATCH("T",OFFSET(A2,0,0,100,1),0)-1,-1)					
	A	B	C	D	E	F	G	H	I
1	T	0							
2	H	6							
3	H	-1							
4	H	-1							
5	H	-1							
6	H	-1							
7	H	-1							
8	T	-1							
9	H	2							
10	H	-1							
11	T	-1							
12	H	4							
13	H	-1							
14	H	-1							

Figure 95

Now you are using the formula *only if* the cell above is a "T". That is, once you have encountered a "T", you can start over, and eliminate the not useful values by putting in a -1. Basically, the formula is saying that if the cell above and to the left is a head, put in -1 because you don't want it (a zero would work just as well). You are only interested in the *first* head. You can see from the above figure that the interesting values are in B2, B9, and B12 – there are strings of six heads, another of two heads, one of four heads, etc.

Now you can gather some statistics on these values, as shown below (the formula could just as well have been =COUNTIF($B:$B,F3) instead of B1:B28:

=COUNTIF($B$1:$B$28,F3)			
D	E	F	G
		Sequence Count	# in sequence of H's
		1	1
		2	1
		3	2
		4	1
		5	0
		6	1

Figure 96

10-Variable Linked Cell

This figure contains a simple Forms combobox (not ActiveX):

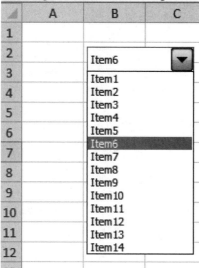

Figure 97

Choose Item5:

	A	B	C	D	E	F
1						Item5
2		Item5 ▼				
3						
4						

Figure 98

So far, so good. But look what happens when you choose item10:

	A	B	C	D	E	F
1						Item5
2		▼				Item10
3						
4						

Figure 99

Notice item 10 is placed in F2, where item5 was placed in F1.

Now choose item 1…

	A	B	C	D	E	F
1						Item5
2		▼				Item10
3						Item1
4						

Figure 100

As you can see, the choices are moving down column F. How is this happening? Well, first look at the formulas in column F:

F
=IF(N1="","",INDEX(M:M,N1))
=IF(N2="","",INDEX(M:M,N2))
=IF(N3="","",INDEX(M:M,N3))
=IF(N4="","",INDEX(M:M,N4))
=IF(N5="","",INDEX(M:M,N5))
=IF(N6="","",INDEX(M:M,N6))
=IF(N7="","",INDEX(M:M,N7))
=IF(N8="","",INDEX(M:M,N8))
=IF(N9="","",INDEX(M:M,N9))
=IF(N10="","",INDEX(M:M,N10))
=IF(N11="","",INDEX(M:M,N11))
=IF(N12="","",INDEX(M:M,N12))
=IF(N13="","",INDEX(M:M,N13))
=IF(N14="","",INDEX(M:M,N14))
=IF(N15="","",INDEX(M:M,N15))

Figure 101

Something's happening out in columns M and N. Column M simply contains the list for the Combobox control, and column N looks like this:

L	M	N
3	Item1	5
	Item2	10
	Item3	1
	Item4	
	Item5	
	Item6	
	Item7	
	Item8	
	Item9	
	Item10	
	Item11	
	Item12	
	Item13	
	Item14	

Figure 102

Nothing at all fancy in N2, is there? But what's that 3 in L1 as seen above?

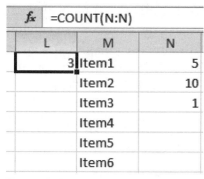

Figure 103

Ah – the plot thickens! L1 is counting how many numbers are in column N, and at this point there are 3, as you can see. So where's the magic? If you right-mouse click the dropdown, and select Format Control:

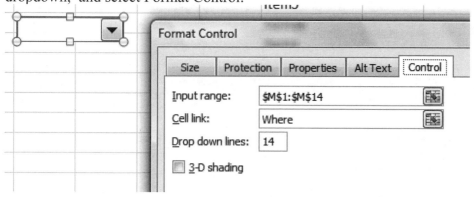

Figure 104

you see that the cell link is a defined name, "where". Here's the definition:

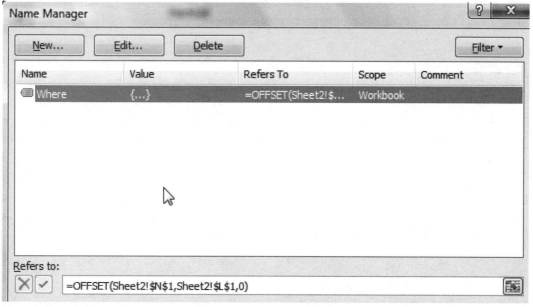

Figure 105

When this is first started, that is, when column F is empty as well as column N, the cell link, where, is =OFFSET(N1,L1,0), and L1 is 0 because that's the COUNTA of column N. So where points to OFFSET(N1,0,0), or N1 itself. Now suppose you pick Item5, as you did earlier. The value 5 is put into the cell link, or N1. This makes L1 be 1, and the formula in F1 is =IF(N1="","",INDEX(M:M,N1)) which picks up INDEX(M:M,5), or Item5.

Next time, "where" points to OFFSET(N1,1,0), which is N2, which makes L1 become 2, and F2's formula picks up Item10, and so on. To begin this all over, you would need to clear column N.

CHAPTER 2 - PIVOT TABLES

11-Pivot Table Anomaly and Workaround

Look at this data and simple pivot table:

	A	B	C	D	E
1	Date	Amount		Row Labels	Sum of Amount
2	1/1/2011	70		1/1/2011	70
3	1/18/2011	5		1/18/2011	5
4	2/4/2011	18		2/4/2011	18
5	2/21/2011	83		2/21/2011	83
6	3/10/2011	42		3/10/2011	42
7	3/27/2011	60		3/27/2011	60
8	4/13/2011	47		4/13/2011	47
9	4/30/2011	49		4/30/2011	49
10	5/17/2011	64		5/17/2011	64
11	6/3/2011	19		6/3/2011	19
12	6/20/2011	52		6/20/2011	52
13	7/7/2011	73		7/7/2011	73
14	7/24/2011	19		7/24/2011	19
15	8/10/2011	68		8/10/2011	68
16	8/27/2011	11		8/27/2011	11
17	9/13/2011	63		9/13/2011	63
18	9/30/2011	76		9/30/2011	76
19	10/17/2011	77		10/17/2011	77
20	11/3/2011	84		11/3/2011	84
21	11/20/2011	1		11/20/2011	1
22	12/7/2011	44		12/7/2011	44
23	12/24/2011	8		12/24/2011	8
24				Grand Total	1033

Figure 106

Suppose you want to group the dates by week:

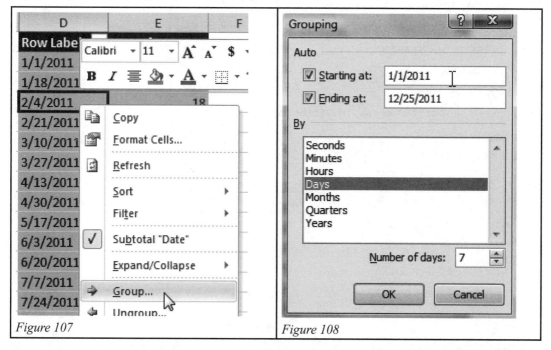

Figure 107

Figure 108

With the result shown here:

Row Labels	Sum of Amount
1/1/2011 - 1/7/2011	70
1/15/2011 - 1/21/2011	5
1/29/2011 - 2/4/2011	18
2/19/2011 - 2/25/2011	83
3/5/2011 - 3/11/2011	42
3/26/2011 - 4/1/2011	60
4/9/2011 - 4/15/2011	47
4/30/2011 - 5/6/2011	49
5/14/2011 - 5/20/2011	64
5/28/2011 - 6/3/2011	19
6/18/2011 - 6/24/2011	52
7/2/2011 - 7/8/2011	73
7/23/2011 - 7/29/2011	19
8/6/2011 - 8/12/2011	68
8/27/2011 - 9/2/2011	11
9/10/2011 - 9/16/2011	63
9/24/2011 - 9/30/2011	76
10/15/2011 - 10/21/2011	77
10/29/2011 - 11/4/2011	84
11/19/2011 - 11/25/2011	1
12/3/2011 - 12/9/2011	44
12/24/2011 - 12/25/2011	8
Grand Total	1033

Figure 109

So far, so good. Now, say you want to have another pivot table of the same data, but grouped by months. Create one more pivot table:

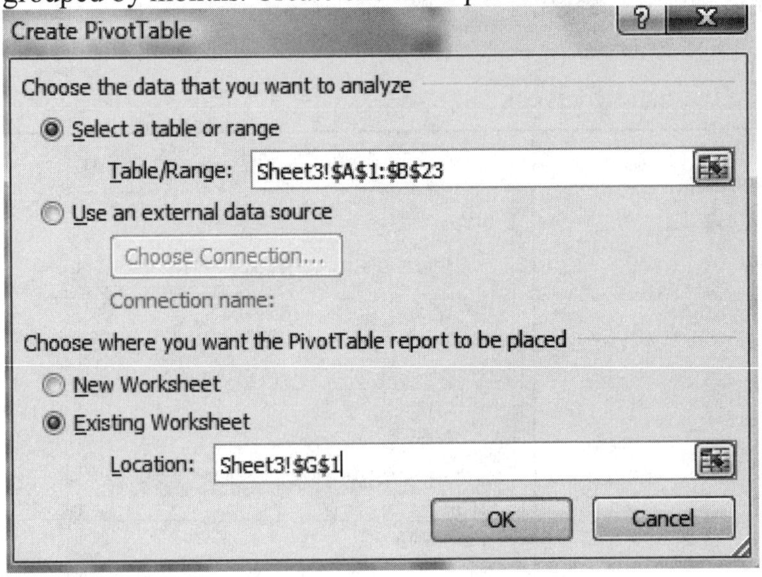

Figure 110

and group by month:

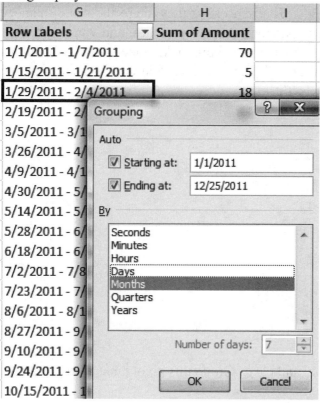

Figure 111

First, notice that this second pivot table already shows the dates by seven day intervals. Figure 112 shows the new result:

Row Labels	Sum of Amount		Row Labels	Sum of Amount
Jan	75		Jan	75
Feb	101		Feb	101
Mar	102		Mar	102
Apr	96		Apr	96
May	64		May	64
Jun	71		Jun	71
Jul	92		Jul	92
Aug	79		Aug	79
Sep	139		Sep	139
Oct	77		Oct	77
Nov	85		Nov	85
Dec	52		Dec	52
Grand Total	1033		Grand Total	1033

Figure 112

It updated the *first* pivot table as well! If you change the grouping in either table, *both* tables will inherit the same grouping. That's because they share the same memory cache. So the way around this is to separate the memory caches, and you can do that easily by temporarily copying one table to a new workbook, make your modifications there, then copy it back! Clear out the new table you entered in G1:H14, and copy the entire table from D1:E14. So first select it:

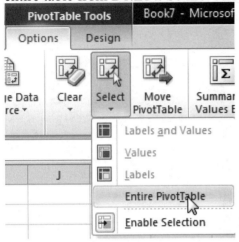

Figure 113

then copy it, create a new workbook, and paste. Group this pivot table by seven days:

Figure 114

The result in the new pivot table:

	A	B
1	Row Labels ▼	Sum of Amount
2	1/1/2011 - 1/7/2011	70
3	1/15/2011 - 1/21/2011	5
4	1/29/2011 - 2/4/2011	18
5	2/19/2011 - 2/25/2011	83
6	3/5/2011 - 3/11/2011	42
7	3/26/2011 - 4/1/2011	60
8	4/9/2011 - 4/15/2011	47
9	4/30/2011 - 5/6/2011	49
10	5/14/2011 - 5/20/2011	64
11	5/28/2011 - 6/3/2011	19
12	6/18/2011 - 6/24/2011	52
13	7/2/2011 - 7/8/2011	73
14	7/23/2011 - 7/29/2011	19

Figure 115

Now copy this and paste it back to the original workbook, and the result here:

	A	B	C	D	E	F	G	H
1	Date	Amount		Row Labels ▼	Sum of Amount		Row Labels ▼	Sum of Amount
2	1/1/2011	70		Jan	75		1/1/2011 - 1/7/2011	70
3	1/18/2011	5		Feb	101		1/15/2011 - 1/21/2011	5
4	2/4/2011	18		Mar	102		1/29/2011 - 2/4/2011	18
5	2/21/2011	83		Apr	96		2/19/2011 - 2/25/2011	83
6	3/10/2011	42		May	64		3/5/2011 - 3/11/2011	42
7	3/27/2011	60		Jun	71		3/26/2011 - 4/1/2011	60
8	4/13/2011	47		Jul	92		4/9/2011 - 4/15/2011	47
9	4/30/2011	49		Aug	79		4/30/2011 - 5/6/2011	49
10	5/17/2011	64		Sep	139		5/14/2011 - 5/20/2011	64
11	6/3/2011	19		Oct	77		5/28/2011 - 6/3/2011	19
12	6/20/2011	52		Nov	85		6/18/2011 - 6/24/2011	52
13	7/7/2011	73		Dec	52		7/2/2011 - 7/8/2011	73
14	7/24/2011	19		Grand Total	1033		7/23/2011 - 7/29/2011	19
15	8/10/2011	68					8/6/2011 - 8/12/2011	68
16	8/27/2011	11					8/27/2011 - 9/2/2011	11
17	9/13/2011	63					9/10/2011 - 9/16/2011	63
18	9/30/2011	76					9/24/2011 - 9/30/2011	76
19	10/17/2011	77					10/15/2011 - 10/21/201:	77
20	11/3/2011	84					10/29/2011 - 11/4/2011	84
21	11/20/2011	1					11/19/2011 - 11/25/201:	1
22	12/7/2011	44					12/3/2011 - 12/9/2011	44
23	12/24/2011	8					12/24/2011 - 12/25/201:	8
24							Grand Total	1033

Figure 116

From here on, since they do not share the same cache, you can change either table without affecting the other as seen in Figure 117:

D	E	F	G	H
Row Labels ▼	Sum of Amount		Row Labels ▼	Sum of Amount
Qtr1	278		1/1/2011 - 1/7/2011	70
Qtr2	231		1/15/2011 - 1/21/2011	5
Qtr3	310		1/29/2011 - 2/4/2011	18
Qtr4	214		2/19/2011 - 2/25/2011	83
Grand Total	1033		3/5/2011 - 3/11/2011	42
			3/26/2011 - 4/1/2011	60
			4/9/2011 - 4/15/2011	47
			4/30/2011 - 5/6/2011	49
		✛	5/14/2011 - 5/20/2011	64
			5/28/2011 - 6/3/2011	19
			6/18/2011 - 6/24/2011	52
			7/2/2011 - 7/8/2011	73
			7/23/2011 - 7/29/2011	19

Figure 117

12-Reverse Pivot Table

(Thanks to Mike Alexander, Excel MVP, for this technique)

Suppose you have data laid out as seen in Figure 118. You want to rearrange this into a table or list which would be useful in a pivot table. Clearly, it currently is not set up right, since row labels in A2:A13 make it not a list. You need to make it look more like Figure 119 (partial list shown).

	A	B	C	D	E
1		North	South	East	West
2	Jan	821	752	530	851
3	Feb	806	344	283	914
4	Mar	279	969	799	925
5	Apr	977	447	530	840
6	May	863	913	944	468
7	Jun	230	949	889	360
8	Jul	304	778	558	722
9	Aug	241	930	856	960
10	Sep	509	747	999	771
11	Oct	972	415	438	693
12	Nov	635	984	911	634
13	Dec	365	252	557	593

Figure 118

G	H	I
Month ▼	Region ▼	Sales ▼
Jan	East	530
Jan	North	821
Jan	South	752
Jan	West	851
Feb	East	283
Feb	North	806
Feb	South	344
Feb	West	914
Mar	East	799
Mar	North	279
Mar	South	969
Mar	West	925

Figure 119

In this article you will see you how to do it.

First, you're going to need a feature which is no longer directly available in Excel 2010 – multiple consolidation ranges for a pivot table You can invoke it by pressing Alt+D+P – as you start typing you'll see this:

Office access key: ALT, D,

Continue typing the menu key sequence from an earlier version of Office or press ESC to cancel.

Figure 120

When you press P, you'll see the dialog below, select Multiple Consolidation Ranges:

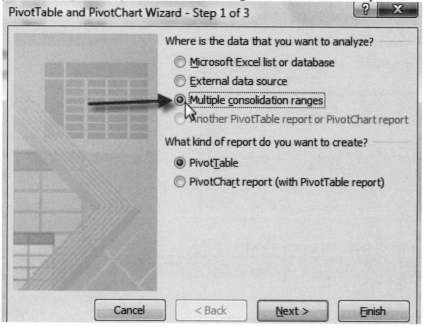

Figure 121

Click Next, and you'll be presented with the dialog shown here:

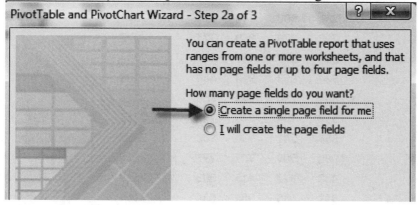

Figure 122

Click Next again to see Step 2b:

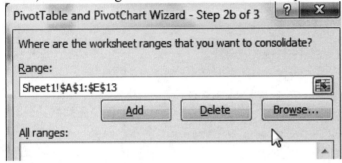

Figure 123

Here, enter or drag across A1:E13 in this example:

Figure 124 (dialog box):

PivotTable and PivotChart Wizard - Step 2b of 3

Where are the worksheet ranges that you want to consolidate?

Range:

Sheet1!$A$1:$E$13

Add   Delete   Browse...

All ranges:

Figure 124

Click Finish to put a pivot table on a new sheet:

	A	B	C	D	E	F
1	Page1	(All)				
2						
3	**Sum of Value**	Column Labels				
4	Row Labels	East	North	South	West	Grand Total
5	Jan		530	821	752	851	2954
6	Feb		283	806	344	914	2347
7	Mar		799	279	969	925	2972
8	Apr		530	977	447	840	2794
9	May		944	863	913	468	3188
10	Jun		889	230	949	360	2428
11	Jul		558	304	778	722	2362
12	Aug		856	241	930	960	2987
13	Sep		999	509	747	771	3026
14	Oct		438	972	415	693	2518
15	Nov		911	635	984	634	3164
16	Dec		557	365	252	593	1767
17	**Grand Total**		8294	7002	8480	8731	32507

Figure 125

Next, double-click the Grand Total in cell F17, to drill down to the details, and you'll see Figure 126 on a new sheet. This is pretty much want you want. All you need to is delete column D, and change the labels in A1:C1 to get Figure 127.

	A	B	C	D
1	Row	Column	Value	Page1
2	Jan	East	530	Item1
3	Jan	North	821	Item1
4	Jan	South	752	Item1
5	Jan	West	851	Item1
6	Feb	East	283	Item1
7	Feb	North	806	Item1
8	Feb	South	344	Item1
9	Feb	West	914	Item1
10	Mar	East	799	Item1
11	Mar	North	279	Item1
12	Mar	South	969	Item1
13	Mar	West	925	Item1

Figure 126

	A	B	C
1	Month	Region	Sales
2	Jan	East	530
3	Jan	North	821
4	Jan	South	752
5	Jan	West	851
6	Feb	East	283
7	Feb	North	806
8	Feb	South	344
9	Feb	West	914
10	Mar	East	799
11	Mar	North	279
12	Mar	South	969
13	Mar	West	925

Figure 127

Now you have exactly what you started out looking for – it's a table which you can leave as one, or change it to a normal range from the Table Design contectual:

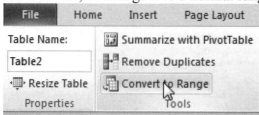

Figure 128

CHAPTER 3 - FEATURES

13-Conditional Formatting

Look at this figure:

▲	A	B	C	D	E
1	436	964	82	561	346
2	427	106	116	928	429
3	965	939	572	843	587
4	664	507	891	13	902
5	398	379	644	2	115
6	873	952	509	184	62
7	289	426	439	716	167
8	165	133	740	257	595
9	441	387	100	608	964
10	440	614	345	14	944
11	904	379	934	540	651
12	662	44	75	259	910
13	944	406	119	843	723
14	864	634	929	598	641
15	223	799	505	837	122
16	290	76	898	985	413
17	294	126	855	262	199
18	997	832	531	930	480
19	496	282	644	334	579
20	48	221	885	907	127

Figure 129

What is highlighted is the largest value in each row. What formula could do this?

You might think this would work:

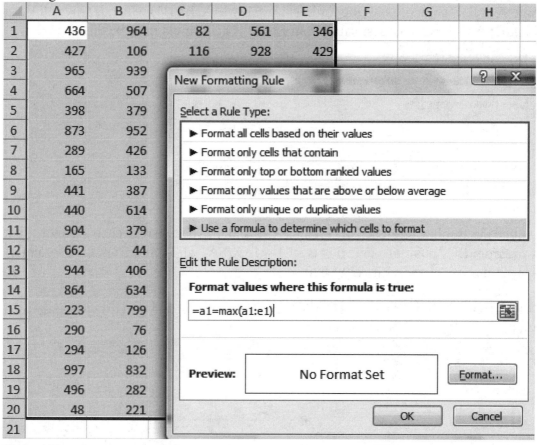

Figure 130

…however that produces this:

	A	B	C	D	E
1	436	964	82	561	346
2	427	106	116	928	429
3	965	939	572	843	587
4	664	507	891	13	902
5	398	379	644	2	115
6	873	952	509	184	62
7	289	426	439	716	167
8	165	133	740	257	595
9	441	387	100	608	964
10	440	614	345	14	944
11	904	379	934	540	651
12	662	44	75	259	910
13	944	406	119	843	723
14	864	634	929	598	641

Figure 131

What's wrong with the formula? From cell A1's point of view, this formula is correct. But from E1's point of view, the formula is =E1=MAX(E1:H1) which is why cell E1 is highlighted – it *is* the largest value from E1:H1. The formula must be this:

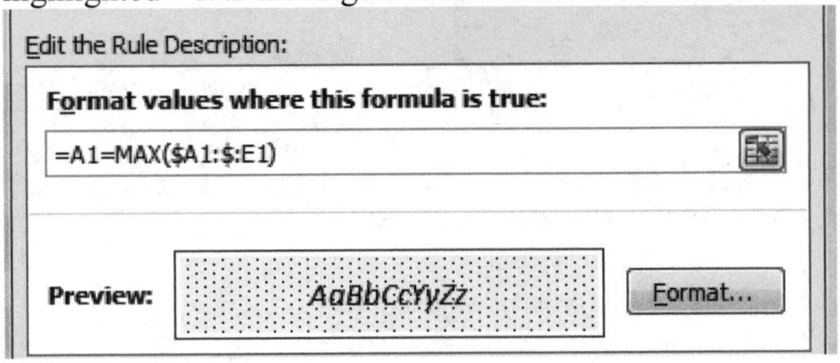

Figure 132

Notice the absolute reference to columns A:E, and the relative reference to row 1. That way, from E1's point of view, this is =E1=MAX($A1:$E1), and from C20's point of view, this is =C20=MAX($A20:$E20).

14-Data Validation on Steroids

Suppose you have a worksheet which looks like this:

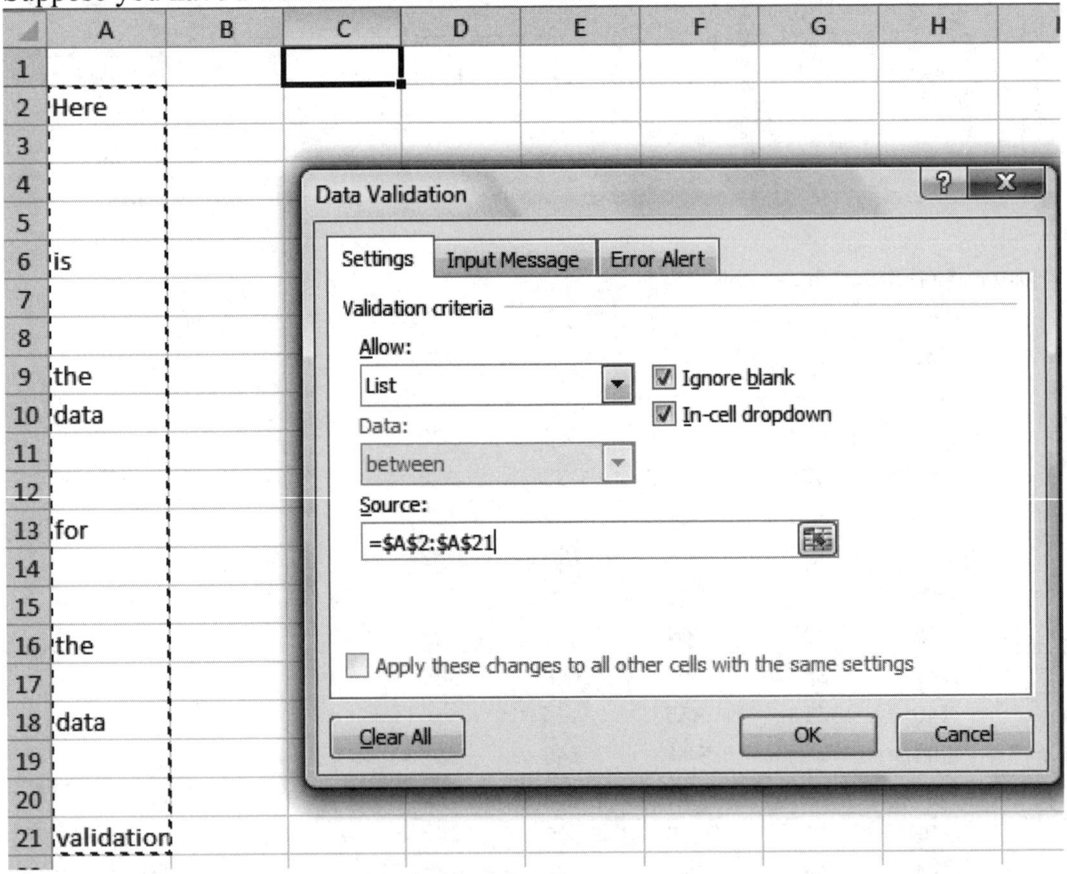

Figure 133

You notice your list has many blanks in it, and after you define the data validation as shown in Figure 133 above, you would see this in the dropdown of C1:

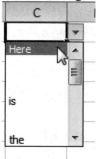

Figure 134

Clearly, that's not what you'd like to see, but oftentimes your real data *does* have spaces in it. What you *want* is the data validation dropdown to look like this:

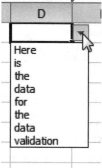

Figure 135

Here's how to fix it. In another area, say column I, you need an array-entered formula like the one shown here:

f_x {=SMALL(IF($A$1:$A$21="","",ROW($1:$21)),ROW(A1))}

H	I	J	K	L	M
	2	Here	9		
	6	is			
	9	the			
	10	data			
	13	for			
	16	the			
	18	data			
	21	validation			
	#NUM!	#NUM!			
	#NUM!	#NUM!			

Figure 136

Array-entering a formula means holding Ctrl+Shift while pressing the Enter key. This is also known as an array-formula. Functions which expect a single value need to be array-entered when an array of values is used in place of a single value. For example, =MID(A1,4,2) would return the fourth and fifth characters of A1, but =MID(A1,ROW(1:6),1)—which is equivalent to =MID(A1,{1;2;3;4;5;6},1)—needs to be array-entered to pick up the individual characters from the first six characters in A1.

By the way, for a fairly detailed explanation of how array formulas work in general, visit http://www.emailoffice.com/excel/arrays-bobumlas.html

The formula in I1 is =SMALL(IF($A$1:$A$21="","",ROW($1:$21)),ROW(A1)), but it's array-entered. The IF-part tests the range with the data for blanks, and if it is a blank, it returns a blank, but if it is NOT a blank, then it returns the row number. Selecting that part of the formula in Figure 137and pressing F9 yields Figure 138:

fx   =SMALL(IF($A$1:$A$21="","",ROW($1:$21)),ROW(A1))

Figure 137

fx   =SMALL({"";2;"";"";"";6;"";"";9;10;"";"";13;"";"";16;"";18;"";"";21},ROW(A1))

Figure 138

Now the rest should be pretty clear – surrounding this with a SMALL(…,ROW(A1)) will return the smallest value, or 2, and when this formula is filled down to row 2, the A1 becomes A2, and the ROW(A2) is 2, so you get the second smallest value, or 6, as you would see in Figure 136, cell I2, (above). The reason you can not use 0 in place of "", is that you would be left with:

fx   =SMALL({0;2;0;0;0;6;0;0;9;10;0;0;13;0;0;16;0;18;0;0;21},ROW(A1))

Figure 139

The SMALLs would be lots of zeros before you could pick up the 2.

Cell J1 contains the formula =INDEX(A:A,I1), so the text "Here" is picked up because this is =INDEX(A:A,2), which is A2, which contains "Here", and in J2 you have =INDEX(A:A,I2) which is =INDEX(A:A,6), which is A6, which contains "is".

An important step is to fill columns I & J past where they make sense – that is, the #NUM! errors are significant and you should use them! Cell K1 contains the array-entered formula to find the location of the #NUM error:

| f_x | {=MATCH(TRUE,ISERROR(J:J),0)} | | |

G	H	I	J	K
		2	Here	9
		6	is	
		9	the	
		10	data	
		13	for	
		16	the	
		18	data	
		21	validation	
		#NUM!	#NUM!	
		#NUM!	#NUM!	

Figure 140

Now this is used in the definition of a name, DVList:

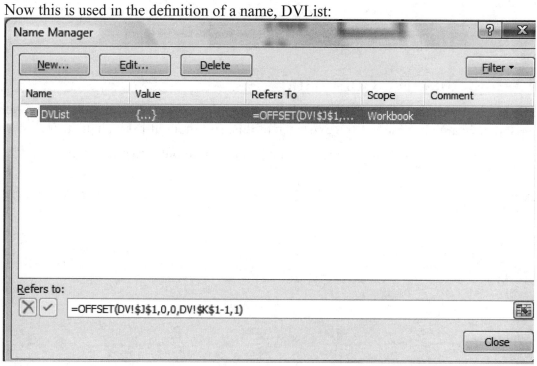

Figure 141

So DVList goes from J1 to J8. That is J1 resized by 8 cells, or the 9 in K1, minus 1.

Finally, cell D1's data validation is based on this name:

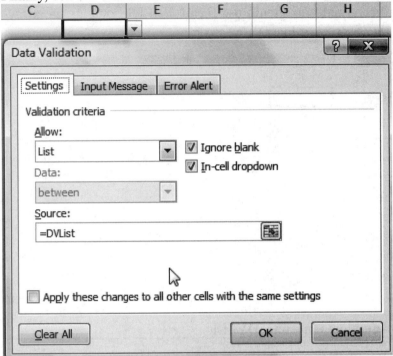

Figure 142

15-The "Justify" Command

Maybe this doesn't belong in this book, because it's nothing special, but I've found most people are not aware of the existence of this, so I thought I'd include it.

In this figure, you have a list of words which you want to put into one sentence:

Figure 143

On the home tab, you see the command you are looking for:

Figure 144

Notice above that the selection includes column Q, not just P.

The result is seen here:

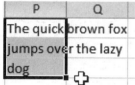

Figure 145

It re-flowed the text to "fit" inside the selection. If "dog" were *not* initially included, the result would be as shown here:

Figure 146

If column Q were a bit wider, as below:

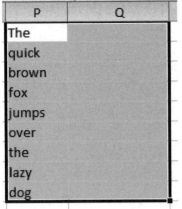

Figure 147

then the result would be as seen here:

P	Q
The quick brown fox jumps	
over the lazy dog	

Figure 148

And finally, if this were the selection:

P	Q	R	S	T	U	V	W
The quick brown fox jumps over the lazy dog							

Figure 149

Then you would see:

P	Q	R	S
The quick brown fox jumps over the lazy dog			

Figure 150

The reverse is also true. If you make the selection seen in Figure 151, then the result is shown in Figure 152 – notice "the lazy" is in one cell. By narrowing column P before the Justify you would see Figure 153.

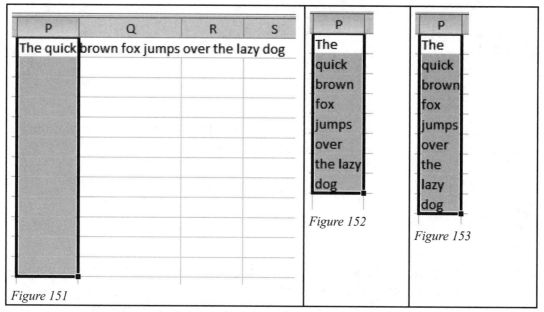

Figure 151

Figure 152

Figure 153

If there were already something below the range:

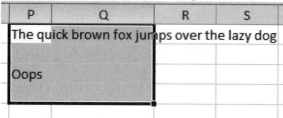

Figure 154

then you would get this warning:

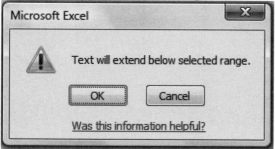

Figure 155

Now you know.

Caution: Justify does not work if the text in the cells contains more than 255 characters. The excess characters are truncated without any warning.

16-Unusual Text to Columns

Suppose you have a worksheet like this one:

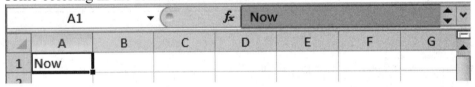

Figure 156

It looks like there's only one word in the cell, but there is an indication that there's more, namely the scroll arrows at the right side, seen here:

Figure 157

The author thinks this would be much better to implement a more obvious sign, perhaps some coloring in the formula bar like seen here:

Figure 158

But I digress. If you open up the formula bar or make the row height of row 1 bigger (or both), you see this:

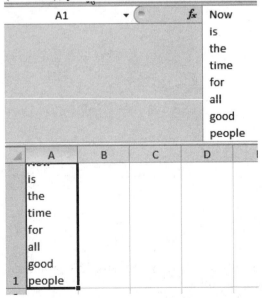

Figure 159

So the question is, how can you parse this out to make it look like this?

	A	B	C	D	E	F	G	H
1	Now	is	the	time	for	all	good	people

Figure 160

Certainly, one possibility is by using non-trivial formulas, but Text-to-Columns comes to mind. The issue is, what character can you put in the dialog shown here?

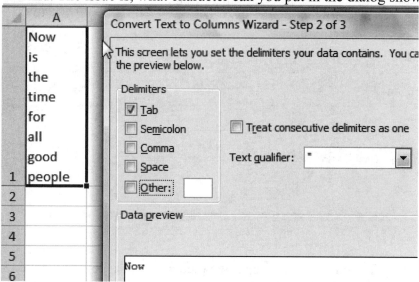

Figure 161

You can't use Alt+Enter in the "Other" checkbox. Strangely enough, if you click in this checkbox and press Ctrl+J you'll see Figure 162:

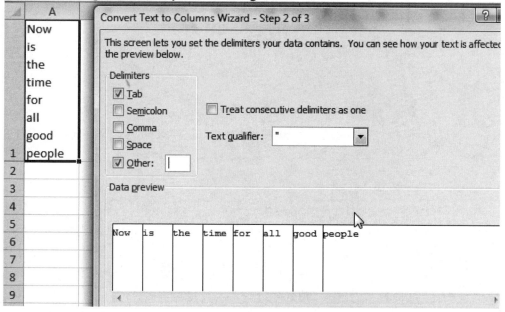

Figure 162

Why? Ctrl+J is ASCII 10 which is Linefeed, which is what is generated by Alt+Enter. You can use it in Find/Replace as well:

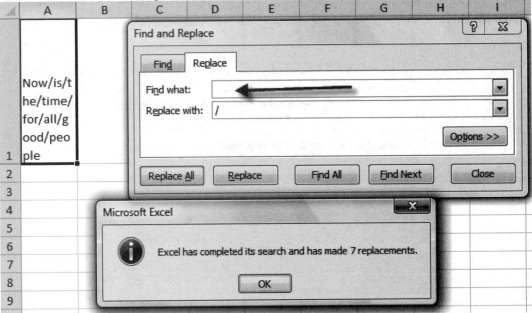

Figure 163

It doesn't show anything in the Find what dropdown (actually it does, but you have to look pretty hard to see it because it's in the second line of the find what box and you may see a tiny dot showing the top of the cursor!), but Ctrl+J was pressed when the cursor was in the cell. The Alt+Enter was replaced with a slash in this example.

CHAPTER 4 - FORMULAS

17-Interesting Formula using MATCH and OFFSET

Look at this figure:

	A	B	C
1	Key #	TOTAL	% of Total
2	14422	800	60%
3	14422	60	4%
4	14422	180	13%
5	14422	300	22%
6	14422 Total	1340	100%
7	17988	720	75%
8	17988	240	25%
9	17988 Total	960	100%
10	26356	103	4%
11	26356	562	21%
12	26356	184	7%
13	26356	181	7%
14	26356	211	8%
15	26356	802	30%
16	26356	304	11%
17	26356	364	13%
18	26356 Total	2711	100%

Figure 164

It has some Key numbers in column A and a value in column B, and each section has a total line as seen in rows 6, 9, and 17. Column C is a percentage of the total for the relevant field. The values in C2:C6 refer to the 1,340 in B6, the values in C7:C9 refer to the 960 in B9, and the rest refer to the 2711 in B17. This article is about the formula in column C, which is a *single* formula that was filled down from C2 to C17. The tricky part is how does it divide by the appropriate total?

The first step is identifying where the total is, and then you can actually use a wildcard MATCH to look for the word "Total" in column A. What's a wildcard MATCH? Something like =MATCH("*Total ",…) will do. Notice the asterisk before the word Total – this would look for anything which *ends* in Total. It's time to look at the formula and see what's going on.

	C2	▼	fx	=B2/INDEX(B:B,MATCH("*Total",OFFSET(A2,0,0,100,1),0)+ROW()-1)						
	A	B	C	D	E	F	G	H	I	J
1	Key #	TOTAL	% of Total							
2	14422	800	60%							
3	14422	60	4%							
4	14422	180	13%							
5	14422	300	22%							
6	14422 Total	1340	100%							
7	17988	720	75%							

Figure 165

As you can see, the formula in C2 is:

=B2/INDEX(B:B,MATCH("*Total",OFFSET(A2,0,0,100,1),0)+ROW()-1)

First look at the MATCH part in cell C2. It's looking for anything ending in "Total" in the range which is an OFFSET of A2 for the next 100 rows. The 100 is somewhat arbitrary – could be longer if it's a possibility that there won't be another Total for over 100 rows. This will return a 5:

fx =B2/INDEX(B:B,MATCH("*Total",OFFSET(A2,0,0,100,1),0)+ROW()-1)

Figure 166

becomes:

fx =B2/INDEX(B:B,5+ROW()-1)

Figure 167

when F9 is pressed. Now you are adjusting this value by the row the formula is entered in, row 2, so 5+2-1 is 6, and now you have:

fx =B2/INDEX(B:B,{6})

Figure 168

So this is B2 divided by B6, or 800 divided by 1340, or 60%.

Look at C3 in this figure:

	C3	▼	fx	=B3/INDEX(B:B,MATCH("*Total",OFFSET(A3,0,0,100,1),0)+ROW()-1)						
	A	B	C	D	E	F	G	H	I	J
1	Key #	TOTAL	% of Total							
2	14422	800	60%							
3	14422	60	4%							
4	14422	180	13%							

Figure 169

This time the MATCH returns 4, because it's looking at a range starting with A3, not A2. The ROW() here will return 3, so you have 4+3-1 or 6 again:

Figure 170

In C4, you can see the MATCH will return a 3 because the range starts in A4, and the ROW() is 4, so the INDEX is for 3+4-1, or 6 yet again. This continues through cell C6 where the MATCH returns 1, the ROW() returns 6, and the calculation is 1+6-1 or still 6!

One more examination and you'll really see how this is working. Look at C7: the MATCH returns 3:

Figure 171

Now you should be passing 3+7-1 to the INDEX, or 9, which is where the next Total row is.

18-Using LARGE (or SMALL, etc) on Non-contiguous Ranges

If you wanted to take the second largest value from A1, B2, C3, D4, and E5, you might be tempted to try =LARGE(A1,B2,C2,D4,E5,2) but you'd get the message shown:

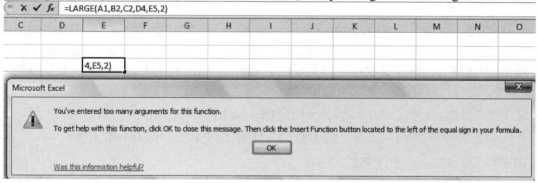

Figure 172

However, if you enclose the references inside another set of parentheses, it works fine:

	A	B	C	D	E	F
1	23					
2		34	45			
3					52	
4				52		
5					62	

E3 · fx =LARGE((A1,B2,C2,D4,E5),2)

Figure 173

19-Using SUMPRODUCT for Filtered or Hidden rows

Suppose you have a worksheet like the one:

	F2		fx	=SUMPRODUCT(N(A2:A18=2010),N(C2:C18="South"),B2:B18)						
	A	B	C	D	E	F	G	H	I	J	K
1	Year	Amount	Region			Total amounts for 2010/South (normal)					
2	2010	100	East			1000					
3	2011	47	East								
4	2009	149	North			Total amounts for 2010/South for *filtered* cells					
5	2007	163	East			1000					
6	2007	219	North								
7	2008	244	West			Total amounts for 2010/South for *visible or filtered* cells					
8	2010	600	North			1000					
9	2010	900	North								
10	2010	100	South		<===						
11	2008	416	West								
12	2010	200	South		<===						
13	2012	521	West								
14	2009	522	East								
15	2010	300	South		<===						
16	2007	563	East								
17	2011	598	East								
18	2010	400	South		<===						

Figure 174

The formula in F2 is =SUMPRODUCT(N(A2:A18=2010),N(C2:C18="South"),B2 :B18) which basically sums all the amounts where the year is 2010 and the Region is South. The N-function changes TRUE to 1 and FALSE to 0. Expanded, the formula evaluates to

=SUMPRODUCT({1;0;0;0;0;0;1;1;1;0;1;0;0;1;0;0;1},

{0;0;0;0;0;0;0;0;1;0;1;0;0;1;0;0;1},{100;47;149;163;219;244;600;900;100;

416;200;521;522;300;563;598;400}).

When the corresponding values are multiplied together it adds up the values in C10, C12, C15, and C18. This is nothing new.

What if the list were filtered, as in this figure:

	F2		▾		f_x	=SUMPRODUCT(N(A2:A18=2010),N(C2:C18="South"),B2:B18)					
▲	A	B	C	D	E	F	G	H	I	J	K
1	Year ▾	Amoun ▾	Region ▾			Total amounts for 2010/South (normal)					
2	2010	100	East			1000					
3	2011	47	East								
4	2009	149	North			Total amounts for 2010/South for *filtered* cells					
5	2007	163	East			400					
6	2007	219	North								
7	2008	244	West			Total amounts for 2010/South for *visible or filtered* cells					
8	2010	600	North			400					
9	2010	900	North								
10	2010	100	South		<===						
11	2008	416	West								
13	2012	521	West								
14	2009	522	East								
15	2010	300	South		<===						
16	2007	563	East								
17	2011	598	East								

Figure 175

Notice that the filter removed rows 12 and 18. Now the value in F2 is wrong, because it doesn't take into account the fact that these rows are no longer "applicable" – it still shows 1000. You can see that F5 and F8 both show the correct value, 400. How this is achieved will be shown in a moment. Let's have a further look at Figure 176, where there is *no* filtering, but rows 11 thru 16 were simply hidden:

▲	A	B	C	D	E	F	G	H	I	J	K
1	Year	Amount	Region			Total amounts for 2010/South (normal)					
2	2010	100	East			1000					
3	2011	47	East								
4	2009	149	North			Total amounts for 2010/South for *filtered* cells					
5	2007	163	East			1000					
6	2007	219	North								
7	2008	244	West			Total amounts for 2010/South for *visible or filtered* cells					
8	2010	600	North			500					
9	2010	900	North								
10	2010	100	South		<===						
17	2011	598	East								
18	2010	400	South		<===						
19											

Figure 176

Now both F2 and F5 are not taking into account that the rows are hidden, but cell F8 shows the correct value. You can see from the comments in F4 and F7 what's going on.

Examine the formula in F8 in this figure:

| | F8 | ▼ | fx | =SUMPRODUCT(SUBTOTAL(103,OFFSET(A2,ROW($A$2:$A$18)-ROW(A2),0)), |
| | | | | N(A2:A18=2010),N(C2:C18="South"),B2:B18) |

⊿	A	B	C	D	E	F	G	H	I	J	K
1	Year	Amount	Region			**Total amounts for 2010/South (normal)**					
2	2010	100	East			1000					
3	2011	47	East								
4	2009	149	North			**Total amounts for 2010/South for _filtered_ cells**					
5	2007	163	East			1000					
6	2007	219	North								
7	2008	244	West			**Total amounts for 2010/South for _visible or filtered_ cells**					
8	2010	600	North			500					
9	2010	900	North								

Figure 177

=SUMPRODUCT(SUBTOTAL(103,OFFSET(A2,ROW($A$2:$A$18)-ROW(A2),0)),N(A2:A18=2010), N(C2:C18="South"),B2:B18)

In addition to the first formula (under Figure 175), there's one more parameter: SUBTOTAL(103,OFFSET(A2,ROW($A$2:$A$18)-ROW(A2),0))

When the SUBTOTAL function's first parameter is in the range 1-11 it includes hidden items but not filtered items, and when it's in the range 101-111 it includes only items which are visible. In other words, rows which are not shown due to *filtering* will be ignored by 1-11, but will include rows which are hidden manually. Whereas 101-111 will ignore hidden rows whether by filtering or manually.

So still, how does this work?

Firstly, a quick look at the options for the first parameter. SUBTOTAL(3,...) (used in cell cell F5) is for COUNTA and SUBTOTAL(103,...) is also for COUNTA but for visible cells! The rest are seen here:

FUNCTION_NUM (INCLUDES HIDDEN VALUES)	FUNCTION_NUM (IGNORES HIDDEN VALUES)	FUNCTION
1	101	AVERAGE
2	102	COUNT
3	103	COUNTA
4	104	MAX
5	105	MIN
6	106	PRODUCT
7	107	STDEV
8	108	STDEVP
9	109	SUM
10	110	VAR
11	111	VARP

Figure 178

You can't use a simple SUBTOTAL(103,A2:A18) because this returns a single value and that then returns a #VALUE! error inside the SUMPRODUCT formula:

| f_x | =SUMPRODUCT(SUBTOTAL(103,A2:A18),N(A2:A18=2010),N(C2:C18="South"),B2:B18) |

D	E	F	G	H	I	J	K	L
		Total amounts for 2010/South (normal)						
		#VALUE!						

Figure 179

It does so because the single value (17 in this case, if no rows are hidden) is inconsistent with the parameters of the SUMPRODUCT formula – each part must be the same size.

The part of the formula which is ROW($A$2:$A$18)-ROW(A2) winds up being {2,3,4,5...,16,17,18} minus 2, or {0,1,2,...14,15,16}. This *could* have been done with simply ROW(1:17)-1, but the reference to the range is a bit more understandable.

So, SUBTOTAL(103,OFFSET(A2,...,0)) will give 1's and 0's for the COUNTA. In this case, it's {1;1;1;1;1;1;1;1;1;0;0;0;0;0;0;1;1}. The 1's represent the rows which show, and the 0's the hidden rows (rows 11 thru 16). These 1's and 0's are part of the multiplier, so any hidden rows are zeroed out.

The formula in F5 is the exact same, but SUBTOTAL(3,... is used instead of SUBTO-TAL(103....

20-VLOOKUP with Multiple Answers

Examine this figure:

	A	B	C
1	Region	Date	Amount
2	North	2/13/2011	$ 4,088.76
3	South	11/24/2011	$ 6,197.77
4	East	10/1/2011	$ 753.31
5	North	2/7/2011	$ 2,058.76
6	West	10/30/2011	$ 2,697.21
7	West	5/13/2011	$ 5,967.93
8	North	12/11/2011	$ 1,369.97
9	East	1/28/2011	$ 9,530.19
10	South	8/19/2011	$ 3,180.17
11	South	9/5/2011	$ 6,616.29
12	East	12/1/2011	$ 2,556.58
13	West	6/26/2011	$ 5,079.40
14	South	1/13/2011	$ 7,109.25
15	North	9/16/2011	$ 9,332.72
16	East	12/17/2011	$ 606.67

Figure 180

Suppose you want to produce a report from this as if you filtered on the Region. That is, if you filter on North, you would see:

	A	B	C
1	Region	Date	Amount
2	North	2/13/2011	$ 4,088.76
5	North	2/7/2011	$ 2,058.76
8	North	12/11/2011	$ 1,369.97
15	North	9/16/2011	$ 9,332.72
18			

Figure 181

But what if you wanted a formula-based version of the same thing?

Here's the result you are looking for in columns I:K:

I	J	K
Region	Date	Amount
North	2/13/2011	$4,088.76
North	2/7/2011	$2,058.76
North	12/11/2011	$1,369.97
North	9/16/2011	$9,332.72

Figure 182

Clearly it's the same report, but there are no filtered items here. If you wanted a new report on East, it'd be nice to simply change the value in G1 to East:

G	H	I	J	K
East		Region	Date	Amount
		East	10/1/2011	$ 753.31
		East	1/28/2011	$9,530.19
		East	12/1/2011	$2,556.58
		East	12/17/2011	$ 606.67

Figure 183

Here's how it's done. First of all, it's *not* done using VLOOKUP. So I lied about the title of this technique!

Column F was not shown before, and it can be hidden (or moved somewhere else so it doesn't interfere with the report).

=MATCH($G$1,OFFSET($A$1,F1,0,1000,1),0)+F1

	D	E	F	G	H	I	J	K
▼				North		Region	Date	Amount
76			2			East	10/1/2011	$ 753.31
77			5			East	1/28/2011	$9,530.19
31			8			East	12/1/2011	$2,556.58
76			15			East	12/17/2011	$ 606.67
21			#N/A					
33								

Figure 184

What's shown in column F is the row numbers of where G1 is found in column A; that is, what rows contain the value "North"? This technique involves using the cell above, so it must begin in at least row 2. It matches the value "North" against column A, but instead of the entire column, use an OFFSET function: OFFSET($A$1,F1,0,1000,1). Since F1 is 0, this is OFFSET(A1,0,0,1000,1) which is A1:A1000. (The 1000 is arbitrary, but large enough to do the job – you can make it any other number). The value 2 in F2 is where the first "North" is. You also want to add back the value of F1 at the end, but this is zero, so far. The "magic" comes to life in in cell F3. Here you see OFFSET($A$1,F2,0,1000,1) which is OFFSET($A$1,2,0,1000,1) which is A3:A1000. So you are matching North against this new range and it finds North in the third cell of this new range, so the MATCH gives 3. By adding back the value from the cell above, F2, you will see the 3 plus the 2, or 5, which is the row which contains the second North. This formula is filled down far enough to get all the values.

The formula in I2 which is filled right and down is =IFERROR(INDEX(A:A,$F2),""). Why use IFERROR? Where's the error? Notice cell F6 – it contains #N/A (which is why you would want to hide column F) because there are no more North's after row 15. So if column F is an error, return a blank. Otherwise pick up the value from column A (and when filled right, B & C). The $F2 is an absolute reference to column F so the fill right still refers to column F.

21-Reversing a list

Look at this figure:

	A	B	C	D	E
1	Original Llist		Reverse1		Reverse2
2	aaa		hhh		hhh
3	bbb		ggg		ggg
4	ccc		fff		fff
5	ddd		eee		eee
6	111		444		444
7	222		333		333
8	333		222		222
9	444		111		111
10	eee		ddd		ddd
11	fff		ccc		ccc
12	ggg		bbb		bbb
13	hhh		aaa		aaa

Figure 185

As you can see, the original list is in A2:A13, and it's been reversed in two different ways in columns C and E. There are more ways to do this, of course, but this article describes two fairly short ways.

Examine the formula in cell C2:

fx	=INDEX($A$2:$A$13,ROWS(1:$12))

	C	D	E	F	G
	Reverse1		Reverse2		
	hhh		hhh		

Figure 186

It's a straightforward INDEX formula, looking at A2:A13, but the trick is in the mixed reference in the latter part of the formula ROWS(1:$12) is 12, so this is INDEX(A2:A13,12), which is the value in A13, or hhh, as seen. When you fill this formula down to cell C3, the ROWS part becomes ROWS(2:$12), which is 11, and the INDEX(A2:A13,11) is the value in cell A12, or ggg, etc. The formula in cell C13 is =INDEX($A$2:$A$13,ROWS(12:$12)), and the ROWS part returns 1, and the INDEX(A2:A13,1) is the value from A2, or aaa.

The second approach is to not have to hard-code the $12. The range is named, and the name is used in the formula instead, as seen here:

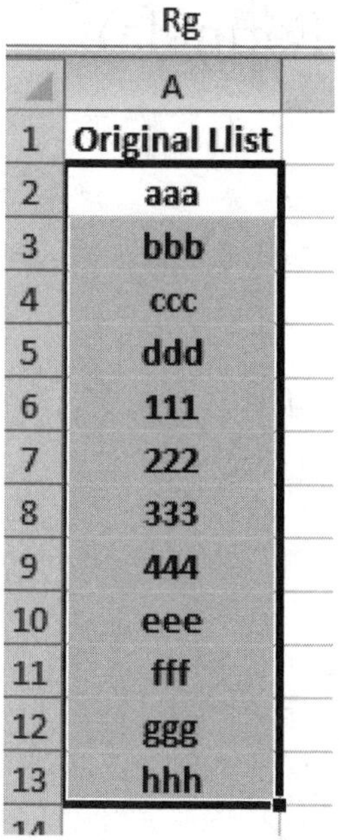

	A
1	**Original Llist**
2	aaa
3	bbb
4	ccc
5	ddd
6	111
7	222
8	333
9	444
10	eee
11	fff
12	ggg
13	hhh

Figure 187

Here, you can see the range is named "Rg". The formula in cell E2 is:

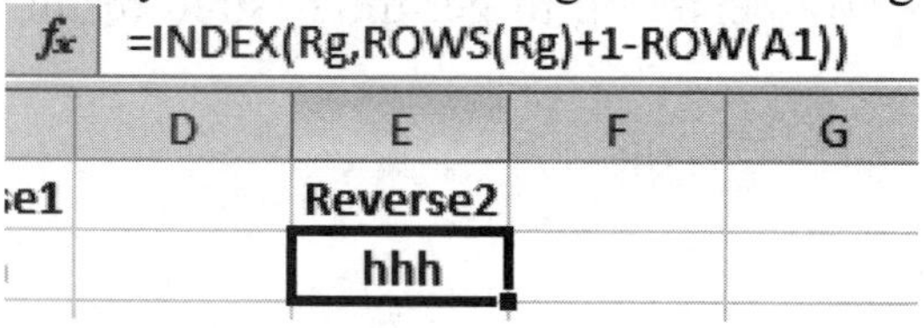

fx =INDEX(Rg,ROWS(Rg)+1-ROW(A1))

	D	E	F	G
;e1		**Reverse2**		
		hhh		

Figure 188

ROWS(Rg) is 12, and this is adjusted by 1-ROW(A1) or 1-1, or 0, so in E2, once again it becomes INDEX(Rg,12). In cell E2, the ROW(A1) becomes ROW(A2), and now the latter part of the formula is 12+1-2, or 11, and the INDEX(Rg,11) is cell A12, or ggg, etc.

CHAPTER 5 - ARRAY FORMULAS

22-Alphabetizing without Sorting (an Array-Formula)

Look at this figure:

	A	B	C
1	NAMES		ALPHABETICALLY
2	Will		Bob
3	Tom		Chris
4	Reed		Eric
5	Bob		Reed
6	Steve		Steve
7	Eric		Tim
8	Chris		Tom
9	Tim		Will

Figure 189

Column C is a formula-based alphabetical arrangement of column A. This approach uses a version of COUNTIF which requires array-entering to get the desired result. First look at the COUNTIF function:

The syntax is:

Figure 190

Where criteria is most often a single value. As in this figure:

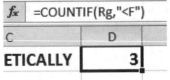

Figure 191

Rg is defined as A2:A9. The function asks "how many items in the range Rg are less than the letter 'F'"? The answer is 3 because cells A5, A7, and A8 are alphabetically less than "F". Another example:

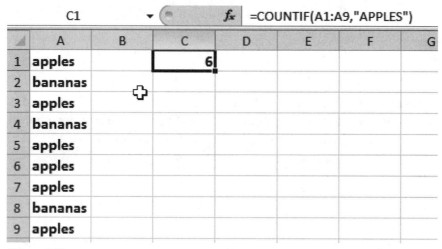

Figure 192

There are 6 apples in the range A1:A9.

If you use a *range* as the criteria, then Excel will evaluate each one and return an array of values. For example, see this figure:

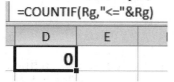

Figure 193

If you enter this formula in D1 as shown, you will get 0. But if you *array* enter it, you get 8 as shown here:

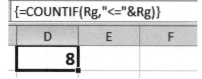

Figure 194

What does the 8 represent, and what is COUNTIF(Rg, "<="&Rg), anyway? If you highlight this part:

f_x =COUNTIF(Rg, "<="&Rg)

Figure 195

Then press F9, you see:

=COUNTIF(Rg,{"<=Will";"<=Tom";"<=Reed";"<=Bob";"<=Steve";"<=Eric";"<=Chris";"<=Tim"})

Figure 196

and each item is evaluated. How many items in Rg are less than or equal to "Will"? They all are! There are 8 items in Rg, so this gives 8. How many less than or equal to "Tom"? 7. Etc.

If you continue and expand the formula in the formula bar (pressing F2 then F9), you will see:

fx   =`{8;7;4;1;5;3;2;6}`

Figure 197

So this is sort of giving you the sequence of items. The fourth item, 1, is "Bob", and is the first one alphabetically. OK, so how to proceed? Look at the answer and decipher it:

	C	D	E	F	G	H	I	J	K
	ALPHABETICALLY								
	Bob								

fx `{=INDEX(Rg,MATCH(SMALL(COUNTIF(Rg,"<="&Rg),ROW(A1)),COUNTIF(Rg,"<="&Rg),0))}`

Figure 198

The SMALL part, seen here

fx =INDEX(Rg,MATCH(SMALL(COUNTIF(Rg,"<="&Rg),ROW(A1)),COUNTIF(Rg,"<="&Rg),0))

Figure 199

when expanded, is 1:

fx   =INDEX(Rg,MATCH({1},COUNTIF(Rg,"<="&Rg),0))

Figure 200

That is, using ROW(A1) in the top row will give the first smallest value, and when filled down, this will be ROW(A2), or 2, or the second smallest value in {8;7;4;1;5;3;2;6}, etc.

So now you match that value, 1 in this case, against the same list of values:

fx   =INDEX(Rg,MATCH({1},{8;7;4;1;5;3;2;6},0))

Figure 201

and this is shown here:

=INDEX(Rg,{4})

Figure 202

or Bob (cell A5, the fourth item in Rg).

Once again, looking at C3 in Figure 203 through Figure 207:

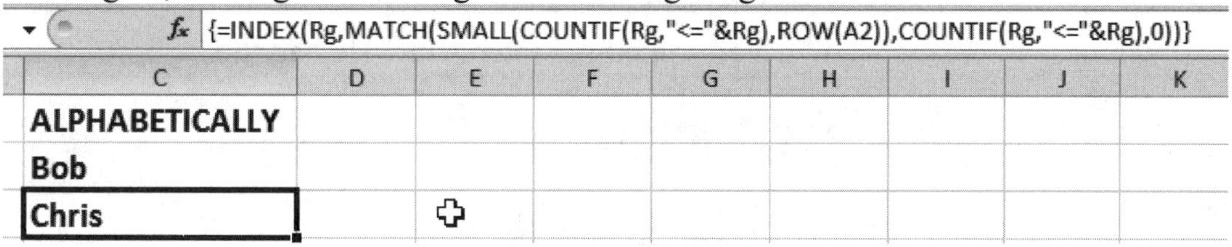

▼ ●	f_x {=INDEX(Rg,MATCH(SMALL(COUNTIF(Rg,"<="&Rg),ROW(A2)),COUNTIF(Rg,"<="&Rg),0))}							

C	D	E	F	G	H	I	J	K
ALPHABETICALLY								
Bob								
Chris		⊹						

Figure 203

=INDEX(Rg,MATCH(SMALL(COUNTIF(Rg,"<="&Rg),ROW(A2)),COUNTIF(Rg,"<="&Rg),0))

Figure 204

=INDEX(Rg,MATCH({2},{8;7;4;1;5;3;2;6},0))

Figure 205

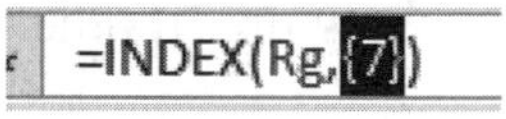

=INDEX(Rg,{7})

Figure 206

Chris

Figure 207

Pretty cool.

23-An Odd Combination

A person once wrote me who wanted something interesting. He had this:

	A	B	C	D	E	F	G	H	I	J	K	L	M	N	O	P	Q	R	S	T	U	V	W	X	Y	Z	AA
																											W5	fx
1																											Consolidate
2						H																					
3						H																					
4																							T				
5														N													
6							S									✚											
7	B																										

Figure 208

He wanted column AA to contain the one column which had data to show up. In other words, he wanted column AA to look like this:

AA
Consolidate
H
H
T
N
S
B

Figure 209

The formula shown here does it, and you can examine its workings:

`{=INDEX(A2:Z2,MAX(COLUMN(A:Z)*(A2:Z2<>"")))}`

K	L	M	N	O	P	Q	R	S	T	U	V	W	X	Y	Z	AA
																Consolidate
																H
																H

Figure 210

The rightmost part, A2:Z2<>"" gives an array of TRUE/FALSE:

`fx` `=INDEX(A2:Z2,MAX(COLUMN(A:Z)*({FALSE,FALSE,FALSE,FALSE,FALSE,TRUE, FALSE,FALSE,FALSE,FALSE,FALSE,FALSE,FALSE,FALSE,FALSE,FALSE,FALSE, FALSE,FALSE,FALSE,FALSE,FALSE,FALSE,FALSE,FALSE,FALSE})))`

Figure 211

The sixth item is TRUE, because cell F2 is not blank (it contains "H"). When this is multiplied by the COLUMN(A:Z), which are the values 1:26:

`=INDEX(A2:Z2,MAX({1,2,3,4,5,6,7,8,9,10,11,12,13,14,15,16,17,18,19,20,21,22,23,24,25,26}*(A2:Z2<>"")))`

Figure 212

You get the array shown here:

=INDEX(A2:Z2,MAX({0,0,0,0,0,6,0,0,0,0,0,0,0,0,0,0,0,0,0,0,0,0,0,0,0,0}))

Figure 213

This is passed into the MAX function, so it returns 6. Now this reduces to =INDEX(A2:Z2,6) which is F2. Filled down, the A2:Z2 changes to A3:Z3, etc.

24-Another Array-Formula Application – Finding the Latest Date from a String with Embedded Dates

<table>
<tr><td>

Look at this odd list of dates:

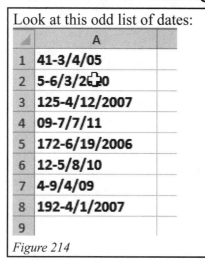

	A
1	41-3/4/05
2	5-6/3/2020
3	125-4/12/2007
4	09-7/7/11
5	172-6/19/2006
6	12-5/8/10
7	4-9/4/09
8	192-4/1/2007
9	

Figure 214

</td><td>

Each date is preceded by some number. Given this list, how can you find which of the dates is the latest? Also notice that some dates have a 4-digit year and some have a 2-digit year. The string lengths aren't uniform, so how can you isolate the date portion?

First, notice that each date is preceded by a dash. You can find the location of that dash and take the last part of the string after it.

</td></tr>
</table>

In this example, the range A1:A8 is named "Range". Look at this beginning formula:

{=FIND("-",Range)}

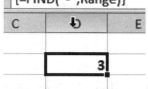

C	D	E
	3	

Figure 215

You can see this was array-entered by noticing the curly braces around the formula. But what does this 3 represent? And why was it array-entered? Look what happens without being array-entered (again in cell D2 here):

=FIND("-",Range)

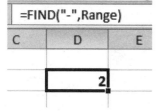

C	D	E
	2	

Figure 216

Why did it change? How could you tell if it's right? What is it referring to? Time for a few explanations.

First, a reference to the range name "Range" in cell D2 actually is the *intersection* of the row it's entered into and the range itself. Look at this figure:

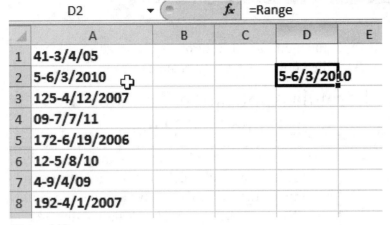

Figure 217

And look here:

	A	B	C	D	E
1	41-3/4/05				
2	5-6/3/2010				
3	125-4/12/2007				
4	09-7/7/11				
5	172-6/19/2006			172-6/19/2006	
6	12-5/8/10				
7	4-9/4/09				
8	192-4/1/2007				

D5 f_x =Range

Figure 218

It's the same formula, but it's producing different results. Hmmmm. How about another look:

B4 f_x =A1:A8

	A	B	C	D
1	41-3/4/05			
2	5-6/3/2010			
3	125-4/12/2007			
4	09-7/7/11	09-7/7/11		
5	172-6/19/2006			
6	12-5/8/10			
7	4-9/4/09			
8	192-4/1/2007			

Figure 219

Interesting. In a reference to a range, where a reference to a cell is expected, Excel returns the intersection. You normally wouldn't enter =A1:A8 in one cell. =SUM(A1:A8), maybe, but not =A1:A8. In order to make sense of it, Excel returns the intersection. As seen in this figure:

	B4	▾	f_x	=A5:A8	

	A	B	C	D
1	41-3/4/05			
2	5-6/3/2010			
3	125-4/12/2007			
4	09-7/7/11	#VALUE!		
5	172-6/19/2006			
6	12-5/8/10			
7	4-9/4/09			
8	192-4/1/2007			
9				

Figure 220

The formula was changed to =A5:A8, and entered in cell B4. They don't intersect, so you see #VALUE!

Well, if it depends on where you enter the formula, how can you guarantee the correct answer? Array-enter it, as shown here:

	B4	▾	f_x	{=A5:A8}	

	A	B	C	D
1	41-3/4/05			
2	5-6/3/2010			
3	125-4/12/2007			
4	09-7/7/11	172-6/19/2006		
5	172-6/19/2006		✛	
6	12-5/8/10			
7	4-9/4/09			
8	192-4/1/2007			
9				

Figure 221

Now, Excel is telling you the *first* cell in the range referenced, in this case, cell A5. Now it doesn't matter where the formula is entered. OK, back to using the named range, "Range".

The first figure you looked at, Figure 215, was array entered, so the 3 is the position of the dash in the *first* cell of Range. If you look at the expansion of the formula bar (selecting it and pressing F9), you see this figure:

fx   `={3;2;4;3;4;3;2;4}`

Figure 222

This series of values is the corresponding positions of the dashes in each of the cells in Range.

OK, so now you have the position of the dashes. The *next* position (notice the "+1" in this next formula) is the beginning of the date, and if you take the MID of the range from that position:

`=MID(Range,FIND("-",Range)+1,255)`

Figure 223

and press F9, you will see:

`={"3/4/05";"6/3/2010";"4/12/2007";"7/7/11";"6/19/2006";"5/8/10";"9/4/09";"4/1/2007"}`

Figure 224

Now you have isolated all the dates. But these are not ready for comparisons, since they're text strings, and 6 would be greater than 12, and wouldn't work, so you need to make them numeric by multiplying by 1:

`=1*MID(Range,FIND("-",Range)+1,255)`

Figure 225

which becomes:

`={38415;40332;39184;40731;38887;40306;40060;39173}`

Figure 226

These are the serial numbers corresponding to the dates. Next is to take the MAX of these values:

`{=MAX(1*MID(Range,FIND("-",Range)+1,255))}`

C	D	E	F	G	
	40731				

Figure 227

All that's needed to do next is format the cell as a date, and you have your answer:

`{=MAX(1*MID(Range,FIND("-",Range)+1,255))}`

C	D	E	F	G
	7/7/2011			

Figure 228

25-Calendar with *One* Formula (Array Entered, of Course!)

Look at this figure:

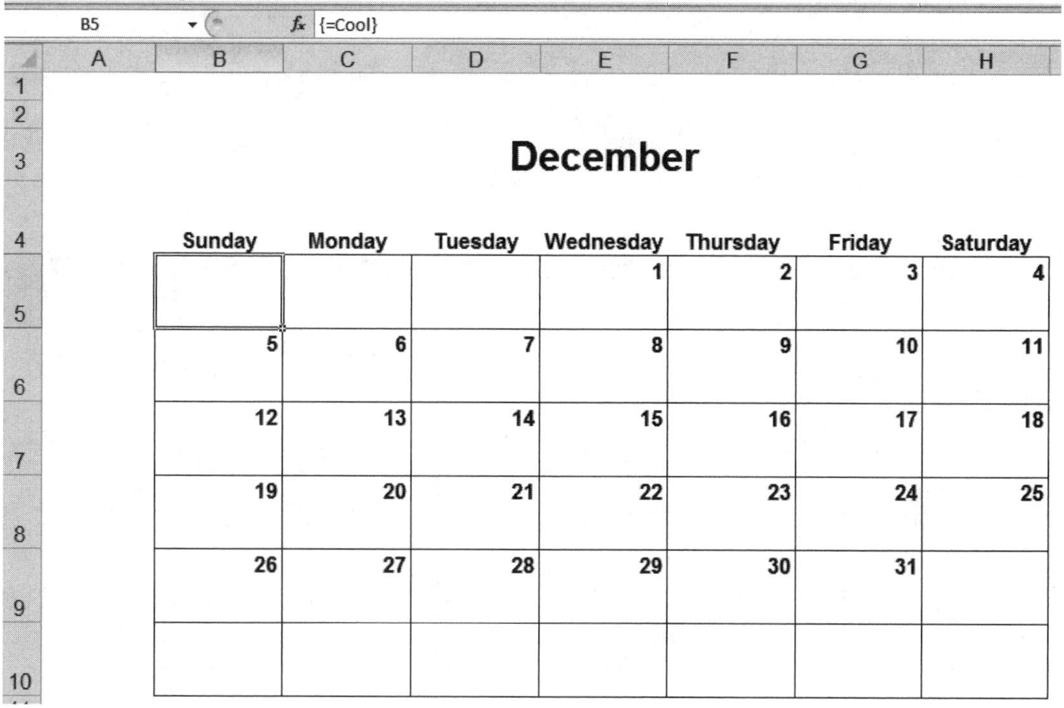

Figure 229

That formula, =Cool, is the same formula in every cell from B5:H10! Look:

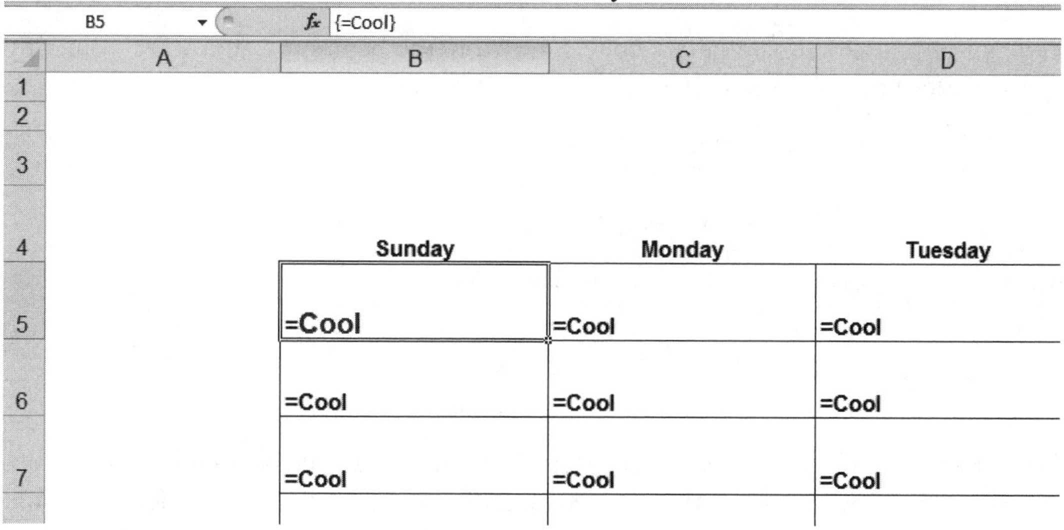

Figure 230

It was array-entered once B5:H10 was first selected. In this article you will see what is behind the formula.

By the way, there's a cell which isn't shown yet which is the month to display. That is, cell J1 contains =TODAY(), (and I'm writing this in December) but if you change it to 5/8/2012, you would see:

B5			f_x {=Cool}				
A	B	C	D	E	F	G	H

May

Sunday	Monday	Tuesday	Wednesday	Thursday	Friday	Saturday
		1	2	3	4	5
6	7	8	9	10	11	12
13	14	15	16	17	18	19
20	21	22	23	24	25	26
27	28	29	30	31		

Figure 231

This is May, 2012. OK, definitely cool! Start from the beginning, and work your way up to this formula in the calendar and see how it works.

Also, assume that today is May 8, 2012.

First, look at this figure:

G1			f_x =A1:C2	
	A	B	C	D	E
1	1	2	3		
2	4	5	6		
3					

Figure 232

The formula doesn't really make sense. It would, if it were surrounded by =SUM, but you want to see what's behind the formula, so you will expand it by selecting it and pressing the F9 key. Figure 233 becomes Figure 234 when the F9 key is pressed.

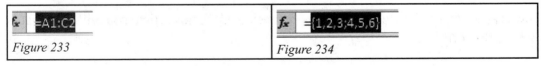

Figure 233   *Figure 234*

Notice that there's a semi-colon after the 3 – this indicates a new row. New columns are represented by a comma. So you are going to take advantage of that.

The number of weeks in a month varies, but no calendar needs more than six rows to represent any month, and of course, they all have seven days. Look at this figure:

	A	B	C	D	E	F	G	H
1								
2								
3								
4								
5		1	2	3	4	5	6	7
6		8	9	10	11	12	13	14
7		15	16	17	18	19	20	21
8		22	23	24	25	26	27	28
9		29	30	31	32	33	34	35
10		36	37	38	39	40	41	42
11						✛		
12								
13					=B5:H10			

Figure 235

Manually enter the values 1 to 42 in B5:H10, and if you enter =B5:H10 in a cell and then expand the formula bar, you see what's shown here:

={1,2,3,4,5,6,7;8,9,10,11,12,13,14;15,16,17,18,19,20,21;22,23,24,25,26,27,28;29,30,31,32,33,34,35;36,37,38,39,40,41,42}

Figure 236

Notice the placement of the semicolons – after each multiple of 7 – indicating a new row. This is the start of the formula, but instead of such a long one, you can use Figure 237 (it may take a while to get your head around this one):

B5			*fx* {={0;1;2;3;4;5}*7+{1,2,3,4,5,6,7}}					
A	B	C	D	E	F	G	H	
		1	2	3	4	5	6	7
		8	9	10	11	12	13	14
		15	16	17	18	19	20	21
		22	23	24	25	26	27	28
		29	30	31	32	33	34	35
		36	37	38	39	40	41	42

Figure 237

Notice that you are taking the numbers 0 through 5 separated by semicolons (new row for each) and multiplying them by 7, effectively giving this:

={0;7;14;21;28;35}+{1,2,3,4,5,6,7}

Figure 238

The vertical orientation of these values added to the horizontal orientation of the values 1 through 7 does yield the same values as shown. The expansion of this is identical to what you had before. Suppose now you add TODAY to these numbers? (Let's assume that today is May 8, 2012):

B5:H10 is first selected and the formula is Ctrl+Shift+Entered:

	A	B	C	D	E	F	G	H	I	J
				fx	={0;1;2;3;4;5}*7+{1,2,3,4,5,6,7}+J1					
1										5/8/2012
2										
3										
4										
5		41038	41039	41040	41041	41042	41043	41044		
6		41045	41046	41047	41048	41049	41050	41051		
7		41052	41053	41054	41055	41056	41057	41058		
8		41059	41060	41061	41062	41063	41064	41065		
9		41066	41067	41068	41069	41070	41071	41072		
10		41073	41074	41075	41076	41077	41078	41079		

Figure 239

These numbers are serial numbers (the number of days since 1/1/1900). If you format these as short dates:

	A	B	C	D	E	F	G	H	I	J
				fx	={0;1;2;3;4;5}*7+{1,2,3,4,5,6,7}+J1					
1										5/8/2012
2										
3										
4										
5		5/9/2012	5/10/2012	5/11/2012	5/12/2012	5/13/2012	5/14/2012	5/15/2012		
6		5/16/2012	5/17/2012	5/18/2012	5/19/2012	5/20/2012	5/21/2012	5/22/2012		
7		5/23/2012	5/24/2012	5/25/2012	5/26/2012	5/27/2012	5/28/2012	5/29/2012		
8		5/30/2012	5/31/2012	6/1/2012	6/2/2012	6/3/2012	6/4/2012	6/5/2012		
9		6/6/2012	6/7/2012	6/8/2012	6/9/2012	6/10/2012	6/11/2012	6/12/2012		
10		6/13/2012	6/14/2012	6/15/2012	6/16/2012	6/17/2012	6/18/2012	6/19/2012		

Figure 240

Clearly not right, but you will get there. What if you format these as simply "d" for the day of the month:

	A	B	C	D	E	F	G	H
				fx	={0;1;2;3;4;5}*7+{1,2,3,4,5,6,7}+J1			
1								
2								
3								
4								
5		9	10	11	12	13	14	
6		16	17	18	19	20	21	
7		23	24	25	26	27	28	
8		30	31	1	2	3	4	
9		6	7	8	9	10	11	
10		13	14	15	16	17	18	

Figure 241

Almost looking like a month, but no month starts with the ninth of the month. Ah, here's one problem. You used J1 which contains 5/8/2012, and you really need to use the date of the *first* of the month. So suppose you put that in another cell:

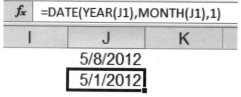

I	J	K
	5/8/2012	
	5/1/2012	

Figure 242

Cell J1 contains 5/8/2012 and cell J2 changes that to the first of the month of whatever is entered in J1. So if you change J1 in the formula of the calendar to J2:

B5 f_x {={0;1;2;3;4;5}*7+{1,2,3,4,5,6,7}+J2}

	A	B	C	D	E	F	G	H	I	J
1										5/8/2012
2										5/1/2012
3										
4										
5		2	3	4	5	6	7	8		
6		9	10	11	12	13	14	15		
7		16	17	18	19	20	21	22		
8		23	24	25	26	27	28	29		
9		30	31	1	2	3	4	5		
10		6	7	8	9	10	11	12		
11										

Figure 243

Closer, but still not right. One further adjustment is needed, and that is you need to subtract the weekday of the first day. That is, cell J3 contains =WEEKDAY(J2). 3 represents Tuesday. So now if you subtract J3 from this formula, you get:

B5 f_x {={0;1;2;3;4;5}*7+{1,2,3,4,5,6,7}+J2-J3}

	A	B	C	D	E	F	G	H	I	J
1										5/8/2012
2										5/1/2012
3										3
4										
5		29	30	1	2	3	4	5		
6		6	7	8	9	10	11	12		
7		13	14	15	16	17	18	19		
8		20	21	22	23	24	25	26		
9		27	28	29	30	31	1	2		
10		3	4	5	6	7	8	9		
11										

Figure 244

And that's actually right for May, 2012!

Okay, You are real close. What's still wrong is the 29 and 30 from April is showing up in the May calendar, and June 1 thru 9 is also showing up. You need to clear these.

You can give the formula a name for easier reference. Call it "Cal" (not "cool" yet). See Figure 245:

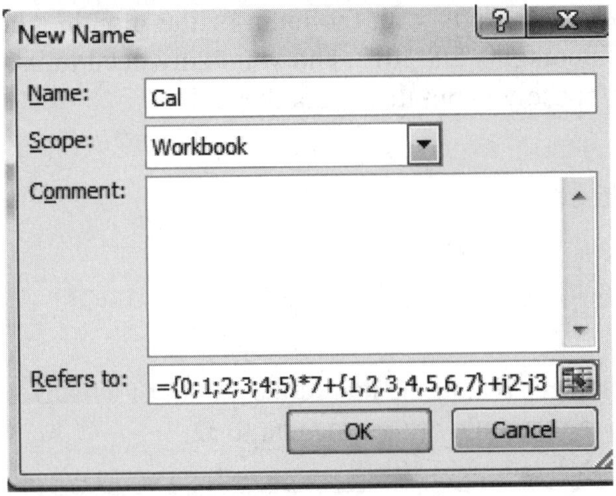

Figure 245

Then you can change the formula to simply be =Cal (still Ctrl+Shift+Enter):

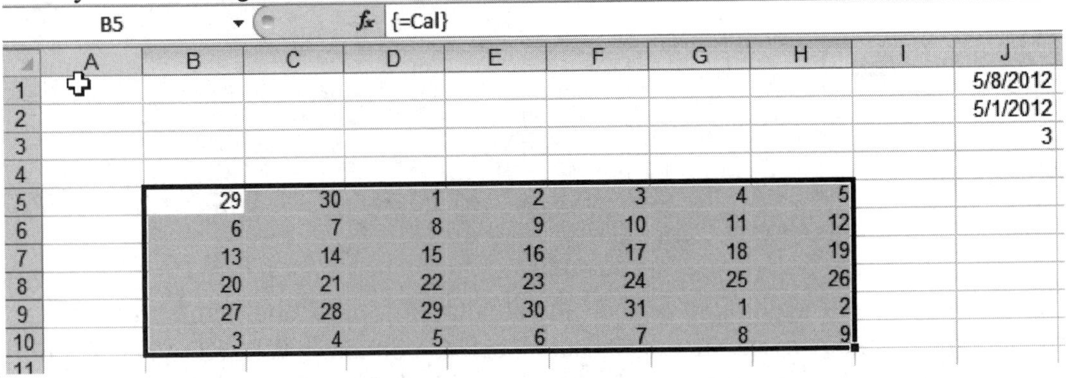

Figure 246

Now you can change the formula to read that if the result is in row 5 *and* the result is over 20, say, then that result should be blank. Row 5 will contain the first week of any month so you should never see any values over 20 (or any number over seven would be wrong – a number like 29 which you see in cell B5 of Figure 246 is from the previous month). So you can do this:

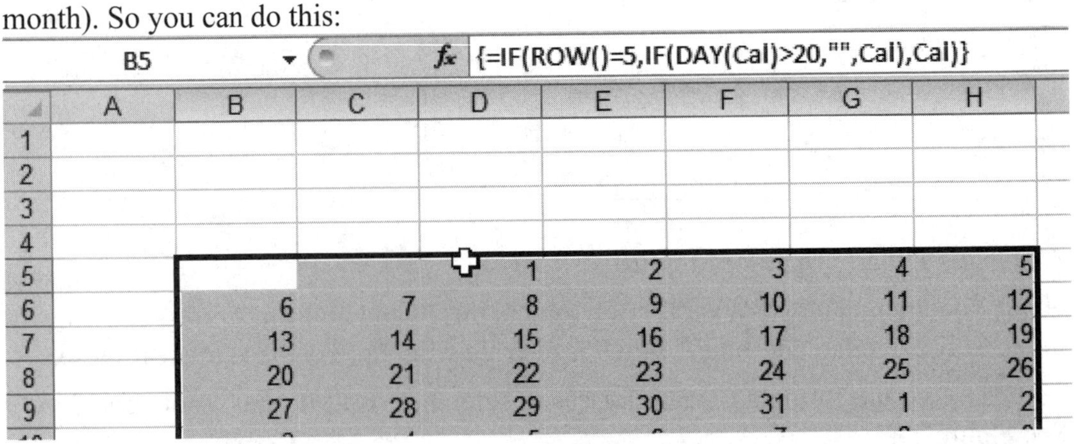

Figure 247

First, notice that cells B5:D5 are blank. The formula now reads "if this is row 5, then if the DAY of the result is over 20, show blank".

You can continue to remove the low numbers at the end – next month's values:

f_x {=IF(ROW()=5,IF(DAY(Cal)>20,"",Cal),IF(ROW()>8,IF(DAY(Cal)<15,"",Cal),Cal))}

C	D	E	F	G	H	I	J	K
							5/8/2012	
							5/1/2012	
							3	
	1	2	3	4	5			
7	8	9	10	11	12			
14	15	16	17	18	19			
21	22	23	24	25	26			
28	29	30	31					

Figure 248

You can replace the last reference to "Cal" in the formula shown here:

=IF(ROW()=5,IF(DAY(Cal)>20,"",Cal),Cal)

Figure 249

with that shown here:

f_x =IF(ROW()=5,IF(DAY(Cal)>20,"",Cal),IF(ROW()>8,IF(DAY(Cal)<15,"",Cal),Cal))

Figure 250

Two things left to do. You can take this formula and give it a name, "Cool":

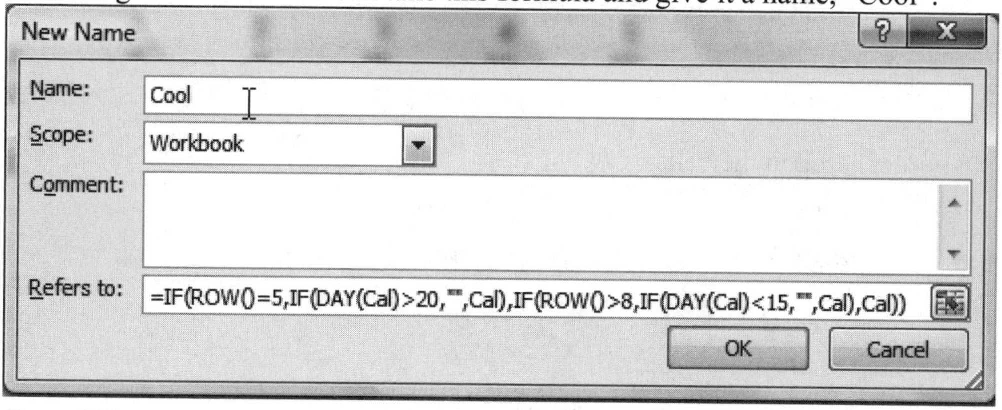

New Name	? X
Name:	Cool
Scope:	Workbook ▼
Comment:	
Refers to:	=IF(ROW()=5,IF(DAY(Cal)>20,"",Cal),IF(ROW()>8,IF(DAY(Cal)<15,"",Cal),Cal))
	OK Cancel

Figure 251

Then use that in the formula shown in Figure 252:

B5			f_x {=Cool}				
	A	B	C	D	E	F	G	H

	A	B	C	D	E	F	G	H
1				✥				
2								
3								
4								
5				1	2	3	4	5
6		6	7	8	9	10	11	12
7		13	14	15	16	17	18	19
8		20	21	22	23	24	25	26
9		27	28	29	30	31		
10								

Figure 252

By the way, defined names are treated as if they are array-entered.

What's left to do is format the cells and put in the Days of the week and the name of the month. So you widen the columns, increase the row height, increase the font size, and align the text:

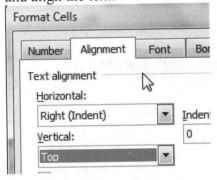

Figure 253

Then put borders around the cells:

Home   Insert   Page Layout   Formulas   Data

Cut

Copy

Format Painter

board

Calibri   14   A A

B *I* U

Borders

Bottom Border

Top Border

Left Border

Right Border

No Border

All Borders

Figure 254

Merge and center the month & year and format it:

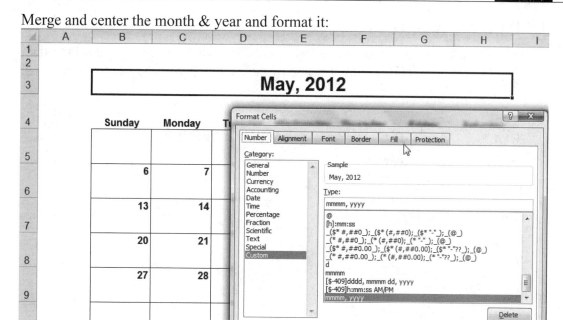

Figure 255

Then turn off gridlines, and voila:

Figure 256

26-Comparing Lists

It's a pretty frequent task to compare two lists to see what's in one but not the other, or what's in both lists. Here examine some formulas which you can use to do just that.

Let's look at this figure:

	A	B	C	D	E	F
1	List A		List B		Names in A not in B	
2	Jerry		Arlene		Jerry	
3	Francine		Bob		Francine	
4	Stefanie		George		Stefanie	
5	Carol		Bill		Jared	
6	Bill		Carol		Tom	
7	Joe		Judy		Jane	
8	Jared		Frank		#NUM!	
9	Tom		Joe			
10	Judy					
11	Bob					
12	Jane					
13						

Figure 257

You have two small lists, called List A and List B. In column E you have a list of names in list A which are not in list B. The #NUM! at the bottom is an indicator that you have reached the end of this list! The formula in E2 does all the magic, and is filled down to E8 in this example. Here it is in this figure:

fx {=INDEX(A:A,SMALL(IF(ISNA(MATCH($A$1:$A$12,$C$1:$C$9,0)),ROW($1:$12),""),ROW

D	E	F	G	H	I	J	K	L
	Names in A not in B							
	Jerry							

Figure 258

Clearly, this needs some explanation. Start with the innermost formula, =MATCH($A$1:$A$12,$C$1:$C$9,0). This is effectively =MATCH(List A,List B,0). The MATCH function *usually* takes one value as its first parameter, and returns where that value is in the second parameter, a range of cells. Here, you are giving a range of cells for the *first* parameter as well, which is unusual, but quite functional. If you were to select just that part of the formula and press the F9 key (evaluate formula), you would see:

fx =INDEX(A:A,SMALL(IF(ISNA({#N/A;#N/A;#N/A;#N/A;6;5;9;#N/A;#N/A;7;3;#N/A}),ROW($1:$12),""),ROW(A2)))

Figure 259

The Match is taking each value from the range A1:A12 and matching it against the range C1:C9. The first four values are #N/A which means the first four values are not in list B. The item "List A" is included in the list. The fifth item in List A is Carol, and this is the sixth item in List B, so a 6 is returned from the MATCH function. The following 5 and 9 are from the names Bill and Joe, found in rows 5 and 9 in List B.

This list is passed to the ISNA function, as seen here:

`=INDEX(A:A,SMALL(IF({TRUE;TRUE;TRUE;TRUE;FALSE;FALSE;FALSE;TRUE;TRUE;FALSE;FALSE;TRUE},ROW($1:$12),""),ROW(A2)))`

Figure 260

Where these are TRUE, the IF-function gives the row#. Highlighting this:

`=INDEX(A:A,SMALL(IF({TRUE;TRUE;TRUE;TRUE;FALSE;FALSE;FALSE;TRUE;TRUE;FALSE;FALSE;TRUE},ROW($1:$12),""),ROW(A2)))`

Figure 261

and pressing F9 again, you get:

`=INDEX(A:A,SMALL({1;2;3;4;"";"";"";8;9;"";"";12},ROW(A2)))`

Figure 262

These are now the row numbers in List A which are NOT in List B. the "" in the original formula is "" instead of 0 because this highlighted list of numbers would be {1;2;3;4;0;0;8;9;0;0;12} and would not be useful to pass to the SMALL function because you pick up those zeros. You *could* have used 1000000 instead of "" (getting {1;2;3;4;1000000;1000000;8;9;1000000;100000;12}) but this is easier to see what's going on.

Now, as you can see, this is passed to the SMALL function, and you are picking ROW(A2) to start because the smallest item, 1, refers to the name "List A"! Continuing to expand this formula, this selection:

`=INDEX(A:A,SMALL({1;2;3;4;"";"";"";8;9;"";"";12},ROW(A2)))`

Figure 263

when F9'd becomes:

`=INDEX(A:A,{2})`

Figure 264

which is cell A2, which is Jerry. This is the first name NOT in List B.

Lastly, this formula *must* be array-entered (Ctrl+Shift+Enter) because you are passing an *array* of values to the MATCH function, which in turn passes an array of values to the ISNA function, and again to the IF-function. Neither MATCH, ISNA, nor IF expects an array of values as the first parameter, hence the overriding array-entry.

To get the names in List B not in List A, simply reverse a few items:

`{=INDEX(C:C,SMALL(IF(ISNA(MATCH($C$1:$C$9,$A$1:$A$12,0)),ROW($1:$9),""),ROW(A2)))}`

	G	H	I	J	K	L	M	N	O
	Names in B not in A								
	Arlene								
	George								
	Frank								
	#NUM!								

Figure 265

The INDEX(A:A... was replaced with INDEX(C:C...;

The MATCH parameters were reversed;

The ROW(1:12) is now ROW(1:9) and the rest is the same.

Lastly, how about a list in which the names are in *both* lists?

`{=INDEX(A:A,SMALL(IF(ISNA(MATCH($A$1:$A$12,$C$1:$C$9,0)),"",ROW($1:$12)),ROW(A1)))}`

H	I	J	K	L	M	N	O	P	Q
	Names in Both								
	Carol								
	Bill								
	Joe								
	Judy								
	Bob								
	#NUM!								

Figure 266

First, if it's in both lists, it doesn't matter which list is passed to the INDEX, but that does determine the other parameters. Here's an alternative:

`{=INDEX(C:C,SMALL(IF(ISNA(MATCH($C$1:$C$9,$A$1:$A$12,0)),"",ROW($1:$9)),ROW(A1)))}`

I	J	K	L	M	N	O	P	Q	R
		Names in Both							
		Bob							
		Bill							
		Carol							
		Judy							
		Joe							
		#NUM!							

Figure 267

Time to examine this using the latter, but you can examine the differences in the formulas in the last 2 screenshots.

The primary difference is reversing the IF(...ROW($1:$9), "") and the IF(... "",ROW($1:$9)) from the previous formulas. That is, instead of returning the row numbers where there is *no* match like you did in the beginning, you are returning the row numbers where there *is* a match. If you got this far in the reading, you'll understand the expansion of the formula in Figure 268 through Figure 273:

=INDEX(C:C,SMALL(IF(ISNA(MATCH($C$1:$C$9,$A$1:$A$12,0)),"",ROW($1:$9)),ROW(A1)))

Figure 268

=INDEX(C:C,SMALL(IF(ISNA({#N/A;#N/A;11;#N/A;6;5;10;#N/A;7}),"",ROW($1:$9)),ROW(A1)))

Figure 269

=INDEX(C:C,SMALL(IF(ISNA({#N/A;#N/A;11;#N/A;6;5;10;#N/A;7}),"",ROW($1:$9)),ROW(A1)))

Figure 270

=INDEX(C:C,SMALL({"";"";3;"";5;6;7;"";9},ROW(A1)))

Figure 271

=INDEX(C:C,SMALL({"";"";3;"";5;6;7;"";9},ROW(A1)))

Figure 272

=INDEX(C:C,{3})

Figure 273

27-Finding the Last Cell Using a Formula

Look at this figure:

Figure 274

How can you determine that cell G11 is the last cell in the used range of the worksheet *by a formula*? Certainly, pressing Ctrl+End will take you there (unless you once had something in a more remote cell and cleared it, in which case Excel still has that cell being the last cell, even though that's wrong . In that case you'd have to manually find the correct last cell (the technique used in this article will show how.) Delete all the columns to the right of it and the rows below it, then save the workbook & reopen it.

Actually, you can delete the rows & columns and execute this one line of code in the immediate pane of the VBE to reset the last position:

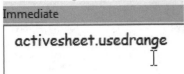

Figure 275

This seems a little odd since you're not setting something equal to this or doing anything but referencing it!

So, how can you find the last column used is G (or 7), and the last row used is 11? You can't use MATCH, since that function uses a vector (one row or one column), and you wouldn't know which one to use! This technique also assumes a reasonable size worksheet. It won't work if the *real* last cell is something like XFD873625! Assume the range to be examined for the last cell is from A1:CZ5000. That should be large enough.

You can check every cell in this range for containing *something* by =A1:CZ5000<>"" which will be a huge array of TRUE's and FALSE's. If you multiply this array by ROW(1:5000) and take the MAX of it, you will find the last used row. If you multiply this array by COLUMN(A:CZ) and take the MAX of it, you will find the last used column. If you pass these values to the ADDRESS function, you will have the answer.

One issue is circular references, because the formula you use will be included in the range. So it's best to put this formula on a *new* sheet. Have a look at Figure 276 through Figure 278:

A1		*fx*	{=MAX((Sheet1!A1:CZ5000<>"")*ROW(1:5000))}

	A	B	C	D	E	F	G	H
1	11							

Figure 276

A2		*fx*	{=MAX((Sheet1!A1:CZ5000<>"")*COLUMN(A:CZ))}

	A	B	C	D	E	F	G	H
1	11							
2	7							
3								

Figure 277

A3		*fx*	=ADDRESS(A1,A2)

	A	B	C	D	E	F
1	11					
2	7					
3	$G$11					
4						

Figure 278

Notice that the formulas in A1 and A2 are array-formulas (entered via Ctrl+Shift+Enter).

If you name the range on sheet1 first, then these formulas are easier to understand. Using Define Name from the Formulas tab:

New Name

Name:	Rg
Scope:	Workbook
Comment:	
Refers to:	=sheet1!$A$1:$CZ$5000

OK   Cancel

Figure 279

The formulas are now shown here:

A1 f_x {=MAX((Rg<>"")*ROW(Rg))}

	A	B	C	D	E	F	G
1	11						
2	7						
3	$G$11						
4							

Figure 280

And here:

A2 f_x {=MAX((Rg<>"")*COLUMN(Rg))}

	A	B	C	D	E	F	G
1	11						
2	7						
3	$G$11						
4							

Figure 281

The formula in A3 is unchanged.

If the range were too large, Excel gives this message shown here:

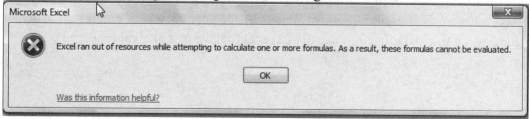

Figure 282

28-Getting Sums from a Text String

For this example, restrict the example to 1-digit numbers inside the text string, and just add them together. See this figure:

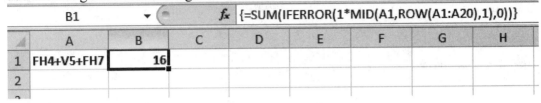

Figure 283

The characters in the string are separated into individual 1-character strings via the MID function:

=SUM(IFERROR(1*MID(A1,ROW(A1:A20),1),0))

Figure 284

Which becomes this:

=SUM(IFERROR(1*{"F";"H";"4";"+";"V";"5";"+";"F";"H";"7";"";"";"";"";"";"";"";"";"";""},0))

Figure 285

ROW(1:20) was used to create a string of values from 1:20, where 20 was assumed to be long enough to handle the string. If longer strings were possible, this would work just as well to use ROW(1:50) or ROW(1:100).

Multiplying each by 1 creates a string of #VALUE! Errors and digits:

=SUM(IFERROR({#VALUE!;#VALUE!;4;#VALUE!;#VALUE!;5;#VALUE!;#VALUE!;#VALUE!;7;#VALUE!;#VALUE!;#

Figure 286

and the IFERROR makes it change from this:

=SUM(IFERROR(1*MID(A1,ROW(A1:A20),1),0))

Figure 287

To this:

=SUM({0;0;4;0;0;5;0;0;0;7;0;0;0;0;0;0;0;0;0;0})

Figure 288

which is now easy to see the answer of 16.

This is an array-entered formula (Ctrl+Shift+Enter), because you are using the ROW(1:20) as the middle argument of the MID function which creates an array of values, when the MID function usually expects to have just one value.

29-Parsing Information Without Breaking in the Middle of a Word (an Array Formula)

Suppose you have the worksheet shown here:

	A
1	Addresses
2	123 Main Street, Columbus, Ohio
3	1554-91239 NorthUmberland Boulevard, Wilkes-Barre, Pennsylvania
4	88 Dogwood Ave, New City, NY
5	

Figure 289

and you need to keep a maximum of 30 characters in column A and the rest in B. The catch? You can't break up a word.

Your first attempt might be:

`=LEFT(A2,30)`

A	B
	123 Main Street, Columbus, Ohi
evard, Wilkes-Barre, Pennsylvania	1554-91239 NorthUmberland Boul
	88 Dogwood Ave, New City, NY

Figure 290

…but as you can see, cells B2 and B3 end in a partial word. B4 was short enough to all fit in one cell.

What you need to know is the location of the blanks in the cell, and find the largest location which is less or equal to 29.

The formula here:

`=MID(A2,ROW($1:$30),1)`

Figure 291

will pick up each character (from the first 30) as an array of single characters. The formula above expands to:

`={"1";"2";"3";" ";"M";"a";"i";"n";" ";"S";"t";"r";"e";"e";"t";",";" ";"C";"o";"l";"u";"m";"b";"u";"s";",";" ";"O";"h";"i"}`

Figure 292

and now you can find the location for all the blanks.

Examine how this complete formula works, using the technique just described:

`{=LEFT(A2,MAX(IF(MID(A2&" ",ROW($1:$30),1)=" ",ROW($1:$30),"")))}`

A	B
	123 Main Street, Columbus,
∋vard, Wilkes-Barre, Pennsylvania	1554-91239 NorthUmberland
	88 Dogwood Ave, New City, NY

Figure 293

First, notice that none of these end in the middle of a word. How does the formula work?

First look at this part:

`=LEFT(A2,MAX(IF(MID(A2&" ",ROW($1:$30),1)=" ",ROW($1:$30),"")))`

Figure 294

When F9 is pressed you will see:

`=LEFT(A2,MAX({"";"";"";4;"";"";"";"";9;"";"";"";"";"";"";"";17;"";"";"";"";"";"";"";"";"";27;"";"";""}))`

Figure 295

Finding the positions of the blanks in A2. ROW($1:$30) gives the values 1 thru 30, and the MID function takes each character:

`=LEFT(A2,MAX(IF(MID(A2&" ",{1;2;3;4;5;6;7;8;9;10;11;12;13;14;15;16;17;18;19;20;21;22;23;24;25;26;27;28;29;30},1)=`

Figure 296

…becomes:

`=LEFT(A2,MAX(IF({"1";"2";"3";" ";"M";"a";"i";"n";" ";"S";"t";"r";"e";"e";"t";",";" ";"C";"o";"l";"u";"m";"b";"u";"s";",";" ";"O";"h";"i"}=" ",`

Figure 297

…and where it's a blank, it again picks up the value from the second ROW($1:$30).

The MAX function finds the *last* blank in the cell, but not one after 29. In this case, 27 is the position of the last blank, so the LEFT(A2,27) gives this value:

123 Main Street, Columbus,

Figure 298

The formula in C2 is shown here:

`=SUBSTITUTE(A2,B2,"")`

A	B	C
	123 Main Street, Columbus,	Ohio

Figure 299

This uses the SUBSTITUTE function to take the 123 Main Street… out of A2, leaving just Ohio.

In the unlikely case that cell B2 appeared more than once in cell A2 you would get an unintended result, so perhaps =MID(A2,LEN(B2)+1,255) might be better.

One question remains – why append a blank to A2 (A2&" ")? Without it, cell B4 doesn't find the blank after NY and splits the cell when it's not necessary because the space before NY is in position 26 and there are no more spaces, so it breaks it at 26:

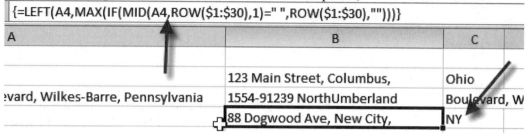

{=LEFT(A4,MAX(IF(MID(A4,ROW($1:$30),1)=" ",ROW($1:$30),"")))}		
A	B	C
	123 Main Street, Columbus,	Ohio
:vard, Wilkes-Barre, Pennsylvania	1554-91239 NorthUmberland	Boulevard, W
	88 Dogwood Ave, New City,	NY

Figure 300

By using A4&" ", it now finds a space in 29, so it all fits.

Don't forget to Ctrl+Shift+Enter or you get a #VALUE! error:

=LEFT(A2,MAX(IF(MID(A2,ROW($1:$30),1)=" ",ROW($1:$30),"")))		
A	B	C
	#VALUE!	#VALUE!

Figure 301

30-Using an Array Formula to Extract a Part Number

Look at this odd worksheet in Figure 302. You have strange part numbers, and the only thing you know about the syntax is it's always alpha followed by numeric. Your task is to put them in *numeric* sequence (assume this list goes on and on). That is, you want the number parts in order, so you wind up with Figure 303 because the values are 5, 45, 123, and 772.

	A
1	abc132
2	part0772
3	abcdefghijk45
4	Pt-5

Figure 302

	A
1	Pt-5
2	abcdefghijk45
3	abc132
4	part0772
5	

Figure 303

In order to sort them, you need to extract the numeric portion of each cell, like this:

	A	B
1	abc132	123
2	part0772	772
3	abcdefghijk45	45
4	Pt-5	5

Figure 304

Now you could sort by column B.

So how can you extract the number? There's no obvious rule aside from alpha followed by numeric. You need to locate the position of the first digit. Work solely with A1 first, then you'll fill the resulting formula down to row 4. "Knowing" it starts at the fourth position (the "1"), but how can you make Excel know that? What distinguishes an alpha character from a numeric one? You *could* look at the CODE value of each character (the CODE of the digits 0–9 are 48–57 – that is, =CODE("0") is 48 and the CODE("9") is 57), but multiplying the character by 1 and if it were not numeric you would get a #VALUE! error, otherwise you wouldn't.

Here's an approach. If you enter =MID(A1,ROW(1:50),1) you would see:

B1	▾	f_x	=MID(A1,ROW(1:50),1)

	A	B	C	D
1	abc132	a		

Figure 305

Doesn't look very useful, but what's *really* in the cell is shown in here, if you press F9 while the formula bar is active:

={"a","b","c","1","3","2","",""...}

Figure 306

The ROW(1:50) gives the values 1 thru 50, and using each of these numbers as the second parameter of the MID statement has the effect of =MID(A1,1,1) and =MID(A1,2,1) and =MID(A1,3,1), etc. Since the MID function expects a single value for the second parameter and you are giving it an *array* of values, you would have to array-enter the formula (Ctrl+Shift+Enter) in order to get the correct result.

If you multiply this by 1:

	f_x	=1*MID(A1,ROW(1:50),1)

	B	C	D
	#VALUE!		

Figure 307

whether or not you array-enter, you see #VALUE! because 1*"a" is an error in either case.

But what's *really* in the cell?

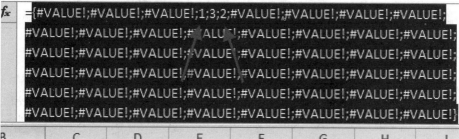

Figure 308

Notice the numbers in here?

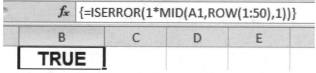

Figure 309

Suppose you test for an error:

f_x {=ISERROR(1*MID(A1,ROW(1:50),1))}

B	C	D	E
TRUE			

Figure 310

And behind the scenes you see:

={TRUE;TRUE;TRUE;FALSE;FALSE;FALSE;TRUE;TRUE;TRUE;TRUE;TRUE;TRUE;
TRUE;TRUE;TRUE;TRUE;TRUE;TRUE;TRUE;TRUE;TRUE;TRUE;TRUE;TRUE;
TRUE;TRUE;TRUE;TRUE;TRUE;TRUE;TRUE;TRUE;TRUE;TRUE;TRUE;TRUE;
TRUE;TRUE;TRUE;TRUE;TRUE;TRUE;TRUE;TRUE;TRUE;TRUE;TRUE;TRUE}

Figure 311

Notice the FALSE values where the numbers were.

Well, now you really have something you can use. Look at this:

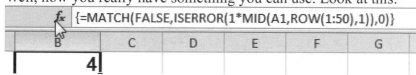

f_x {=MATCH(FALSE,ISERROR(1*MID(A1,ROW(1:50),1)),0)}

B	C	D	E	F	G
4					

Figure 312

Yes, the 4 states the position of the first digit in A1! Very useful!

Without array-entering, you would see:

	=MATCH(FALSE,ISERROR(1*MID(A1,ROW(1:50),1)),0)					
B	**C**	**D**	**E**	**F**	**G**	
#N/A						

Figure 313

There is no "behind the scenes" value! Pressing F9 in the formula bar would also simply show a 4. So you are taking advantage of intermediate calculations in one cell.

Knowing this, you can use the MID function to take out the number part:

	{=MID(A1,MATCH(FALSE,ISERROR(1*MID(A1,ROW(1:50),1)),0),50)}						
B	**C**	**D**	**E**	**F**	**G**	**H**	
132							

Figure 314

The 50 at the end is just to make it arbitrarily large enough to get a large number. Probably 10 would be fine! If you want accuracy you could use ROW(INDIRECT("1:" & LEN(A1)))

But notice this is left-aligned, because the MID function returns a string, and if you want to sort this numerically you need numeric. So you multiply by 1:

	{=1*MID(A1,MATCH(FALSE,ISERROR(1*MID(A1,ROW(1:50),1)),0),50)}						
B	**C**	**D**	**E**	**F**	**G**	**H**	
132							

Figure 315

All that's left to do is fill down. But wait! ROW(1:50) will become ROW(2:51), etc., so you need to change the formula to include the absolute references in ROW($1:$50), then fill down:

	{=1*MID(A1,MATCH(FALSE,ISERROR(1*MID(A1,ROW($1:$50),1)),0),50)}						
B	**C**	**D**	**E**	**F**	**G**	**H**	
132							
772							
45							
5							

Figure 316

Sort on column B!

Pretty powerful stuff. Worthy of study if this is new to you!

After reading through all the above, I had some fellow MVP-ers look over this book, and Rick Rothstein came up with this non-array-formula version to accomplish the same thing! Thanks, Rick! I'm leaving the technique in the book because I think it's instructive. Here's Rick's solution:

f_x	=1*MID(A1,MIN(FIND({0,1,2,3,4,5,6,7,8,9},A1&"0123456789")),99)						
B	**C**	**D**	**E**	**F**	**G**	**H**
132						
772						
45						
5						

Figure 317

Here is how it works:

=1*MID(A1,MIN(FIND({0,1,2,3,4,5,6,7,8,9},A1&"0123456789")),99)

Figure 318

…becomes:

=1*MID(A1,MIN(FIND({0,1,2,3,4,5,6,7,8,9},"abc1320123456789")),99)

Figure 319

…which becomes:

=1*MID(A1,MIN({7,4,6,5,11,12,13,14,15,16}),99)

Figure 320

…which becomes:

=1*MID(A1,4,99)

Figure 321

..which is easy to figure out!

31-VLOOKUP with Multiple Answers – Another Look

Here's another approach for getting the same values in column F in an earlier example. The idea here is to get a list of row numbers containing "North" (or the value in G1) by examining the range A1:A17 all in one cell. Look at this formula in F2:

{=SMALL(IF($A$1:$A$17=$G$1,ROW($1:$17),""),ROW(A1))}					
D	**E**	**F**	**G**	**H**	**I**
			North		
'6		2			
'7		5			
1		8			
'6		15			
1		#NUM!			

Figure 322

First, notice the values are the same as before. The IF-statement shown here:

`=SMALL(IF($A$1:$A$17=$G$1,ROW($1:$17),""),ROW(A1))`

Figure 323

becomes this:

`=SMALL({"";2;"";"";5;"";"";8;"";"";"";"";"";"";15;"";""},ROW(A1))`

Figure 324

when expanded by pressing the F9 key. You couldn't have used IF($A$1:$A$17=$G$1 ,ROW($1:$17),0) because the expansion would be full of zeros, and the SMALL would pick these up first, before giving you useful information!

From here, it should be clear how it works – the smallest value from the highlighted range is 2. When this is filled down, you see:

`=SMALL({"";2;"";"";5;"";"";8;"";"";"";"";"";"";15;"";""},ROW(A2))`

Figure 325

and ROW(A2) is 2, so this returns 5, etc.

To reiterate – this is an array-formula, and must be entered with Ctrl+Shift+Enter. If you had entered this normally, you would see this:

`=SMALL(IF($A$1:$A$17=$G$1,ROW($1:$17),""),ROW(A2))`

	D	E	F	G	H	I
				North		
'6			1			
'7			#VALUE!			
;1			#VALUE!			
'6			#NUM!			

Figure 326

which is clearly not right! How do you know to enter as an array formula? Look at the IF-statement inside. The first parameter to an IF-statement is supposed to be a logical text, which is defined as anything which can evaluate to TRUE or FALSE. If you look at this expansion (pressing F9 with this highlighted):

`=SMALL(IF($A$1:$A$17=$G$1,ROW($1:$17),""),ROW(A1))`

Figure 327

you would see:

`=SMALL(IF({FALSE;TRUE;FALSE;FALSE;TRUE;FALSE;FALSE;TRUE;FALSE;FALSE;FALSE;FALSE;FALSE;FALSE;TRUE;FALSE;FALSE},RO`

Figure 328

which is *not* TRUE or FALSE, it's an *array* of TRUE/FALSE values! One hint to knowing if a formula should be an array formula is if the function expects a single value and you're giving it *many* values to work on. You might think =SUM(A1:A5) should be an array-formula, but the SUM function *expects* an array of values. More array formula examples are found later in this book.

CHAPTER 6 - CHARTS

32-Dynamic Range Names and Charts

Look at this figure:

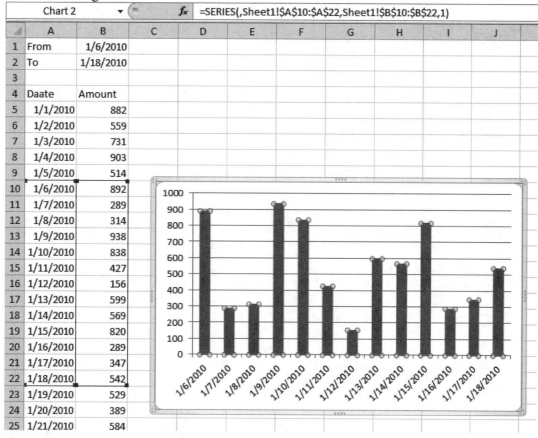

| | Chart 2 | ▼ | | f_x | =SERIES(,Sheet1!$A$10:$A$22,Sheet1!$B$10:$B$22,1) |

	A	B	C	D	E	F	G	H	I	J
1	From	1/6/2010								
2	To	1/18/2010								
3										
4	Daate	Amount								
5	1/1/2010	882								
6	1/2/2010	559								
7	1/3/2010	731								
8	1/4/2010	903								
9	1/5/2010	514								
10	1/6/2010	892								
11	1/7/2010	289								
12	1/8/2010	314								
13	1/9/2010	938								
14	1/10/2010	838								
15	1/11/2010	427								
16	1/12/2010	156								
17	1/13/2010	599								
18	1/14/2010	569								
19	1/15/2010	820								
20	1/16/2010	289								
21	1/17/2010	347								
22	1/18/2010	542								
23	1/19/2010	529								
24	1/20/2010	389								
25	1/21/2010	584								

Figure 329

Clearly, this chart was made from the selected cells, A10:B22, and they correspond to the dates in B1:B2. Wouldn't it be nice to simply change the data in B1 and B2 and have the chart reflect these new dates?

Define a name, called Dates, to be

=INDEX(Info!$A:$A,MATCH(Info!$B$1,Info!$A:$A,0)):INDEX(Info!$A:$A, MATCH(Info!$B$2,Info!$A:$A,0))

The MATCH statements are returning the row numbers for B1 and B2, which in this case are 10 and 22, so the formula is the same as =INDEX(Info!$A:$A,10):INDEX (Info!$A:$A,22) which is A10:A22. As you change the data in B1 and B2 the range called Dates is updated. Another name was defined, Amts, to be the column to the right: =OFFSET(Dates,,1). After all, no need to have to do more MATCH formulas when this simple one can be used!

Next, change the SERIES formula. An interesting thing happens, you select the $A$10:$A$22 in the formula and replace it with Dates,

=SERIES(,Info!Dates,Info!$B$10:$B$22,1)

Figure 330

...then when you press enter you'll see this:

=SERIES(,EOTB.xlsm!Dates,Info!$B$10:$B$22,1)

Figure 331

That is, the sheet name is replaced with the workbook name. Just an interesting thing to notice!

Similarly, when you replace $B$10:$B$22 with Amts, you see this:

=SERIES(,EOTB.xlsm!Dates,EOTB.xlsm!Amts,1)

Figure 332

Now, if you simply change the dates, the chart updates:

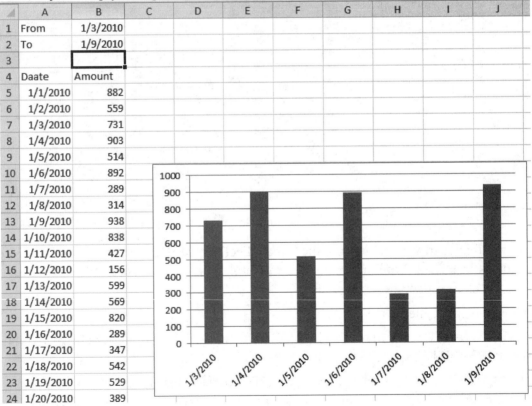

Figure 333

33-More Dynamic Charting

Look at these next two figures:

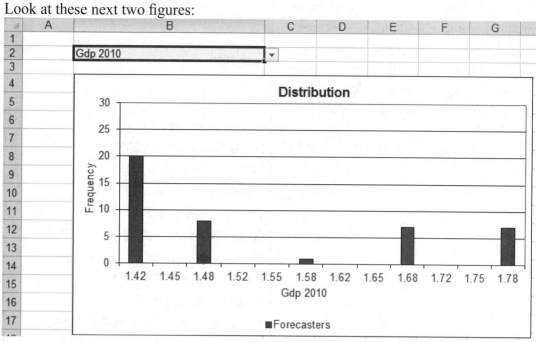

Figure 334

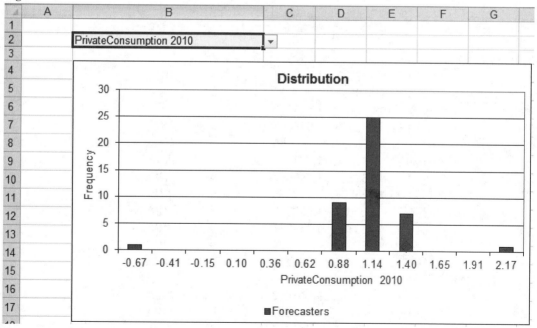

Figure 335

How does simply changing the value in the dropdown in B2 update the chart?

Well, first look at the source of the data validation list. As you can see in the next figure, column T contains this list.

The data for the items comes from another sheet, and has the information in columns D:F, with the description in column A and the data starting one cell below the description. That is, the data for Gdp 2010 is in D32:F43 as seen in Figure 337, and is always 12 rows:

T	U	V	V
List			
Gdp 2010			
Gdp 2011			
Gdp 2012			
PrivateConsumption 2010			
PrivateConsumption 2011			
PrivateConsumption 2012			
GovtConsumption 2010			
GovtConsumption 2011			
GovtConsumption 2012			
FixedInvestment 2010			
FixedInvestment 2011			
FixedInvestment 2012			
ChangeInventoryContribution 2010			
ChangeInventoryContribution 2011			

Figure 336

	A	B	C	D	E	F
30						
31	Gdp 2010					
32		1.4	1.433333	1.416667	20	#N/A
33		1.433333	1.466667	1.45	0	#N/A
34		1.466667	1.5	1.483333	8	1
35		1.5	1.533333	1.516667	0	#N/A
36		1.533333	1.566667	1.55	0	#N/A
37		1.566667	1.6	1.583333	1	#N/A
38		1.6	1.633333	1.616667	0	#N/A
39		1.633333	1.666667	1.65	0	#N/A
40		1.666667	1.7	1.683333	7	#N/A
41		1.7	1.733333	1.716667	0	#N/A
42		1.733333	1.766667	1.75	0	#N/A
43		1.766667	1.8	1.783333	7	#N/A
44	Gdp 2011					
45		0.9	1.083333	0.991667	1	#N/A
46		1.083333	1.266667	1.175	0	#N/A
47		1.266667	1.45	1.358333	6	#N/A
48		1.45	1.633333	1.541667	8	1
49		1.633333	1.816667	1.725	4	#N/A

Figure 337

To accomplish this, a number of things need to be done. If column S is unhidden, you see the formulas as shown here:

S4				fx	=MATCH(T4,Sheet1!A:A,0)		

	O	P	Q	R	S	T	U	V
1					7			
2					110			
3						List		
4					31	Gdp 2010		
5					44	Gdp 2011		
6					57	Gdp 2012		
7					109	PrivateConsumption 2010		
8					122	PrivateConsumption 2011		
9					135	PrivateConsumption 2012		
10					187	GovtConsumption 2010		
11					200	GovtConsumption 2011		
12					213	GovtConsumption 2012		
13					265	FixedInvestment 2010		
14					278	FixedInvestment 2011		

Figure 338

Starting from cell S4 and down, you are picking up the location of the description in column A of Sheet1 (the sheet with all the data). Cell S1 contains the location in the list of the item chosen in cell B2 from the dropdown,

fx	=MATCH(B2,T:T,0)	

R	S	T
	7	
	110	
		List
	31	Gdp 2010
	44	Gdp 2011

Figure 339

and cell S2 contains the row number of the first row of the data:

=INDEX(S:S,S1)+1		

R	S	T
	7	
	110	
		List
	31	Gdp 2010
	44	Gdp 2011

Figure 340

Now, knowing the first row, and knowing the number of rows is always 12, you can define a few names.

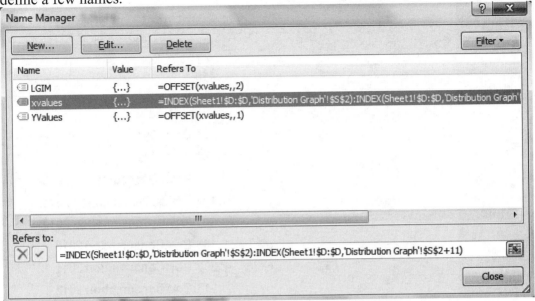

Figure 341

As you can see, the name "xvalues" is set to

=INDEX(Sheet1!$D:$D,'Distribution Graph'!$S$2):INDEX(Sheet1!$D:$D,'Distribution Graph'!$S$2+11)

which could also have been =OFFSET(Sheet1!$D:$D,'Distribution Graph'!$S$2-1,0,12,1) – both definitions refer to 12 rows from the correct starting point for the values in column D of Sheet1.

The yvalues are one column to the right of the xvalues, so the simple definition of =OFFSET(xvalues,,1) does the job, and similarly for the range called LGIM, which is column F.

The last thing to do is name the series in the chart, which uses these names. See the next two figures:

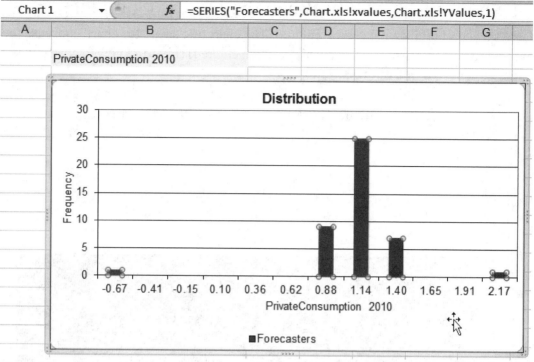

Figure 342

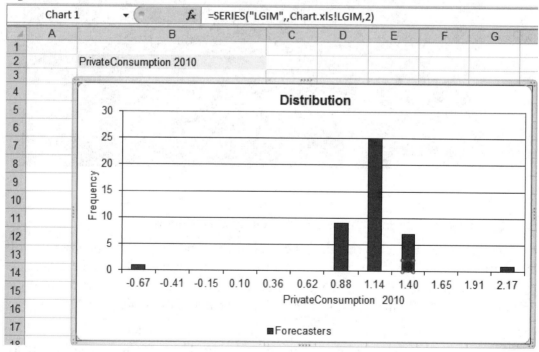

Figure 343

That's all there is to it!

34-Show a Chart Only When the Data is Complete

Here's a chart based on data being entered. The chart title says "No chart", because the data is incomplete (Item 6's data hasn't yet been entered) (if you're new to charting, see a few basics at the end of this article):

▲	A	B	C	D	E	F	G	H
1		Item1	Item2	Item3	Item4	Item5	Item6	
2	12/1/2010	383	355	158	355	246	130	
3	12/2/2010	377	26	159	28	392	157	
4	12/3/2010	75	50	300	122	133	57	
5	12/4/2010	77	58	316	183	150	70	
6	12/5/2010	227	364	371	335	371		
7								
8								
9								

No Chart

(chart with y-axis values 1, 0.9, 0.8, 0.7, 0.6, 0.5, 0.4, 0.3, 0.2, 0.1, 0 and x-axis categories Item 1, Item 2, Item 3, Item 4, Item 5, Item 6)

Figure 344

But as soon as the information is entered in G6, you get Figure 345.

How is this done? In fact, *only* when the data in column G is entered in any row will the chart contain information. That information is the difference between the data in the row just entered and the row above. In this example, the small column for item 6 is the 85 in G6 minus the 70 in G5. Item 2's column is the data from C6-C5, or 316.

Pretty nifty, eh? OK the secret is in the cells which haven't been shown to you yet. The data for the chart in Figure 344 is shown in Figure 346. The data for the chart in Figure 345 is shown in Figure 347.

⊿	A	B	C	D	E	F	G	H
1		Item1	Item2	Item3	Item4	Item5	Item6	
2	12/1/2010	383	355	158	355	246	130	
3	12/2/2010	377	26	159	28	392	157	
4	12/3/2010	75	50	300	122	133	57	
5	12/4/2010	77	58	316	183	150	70	
6	12/5/2010	227	364	371	335	371	85	
7								

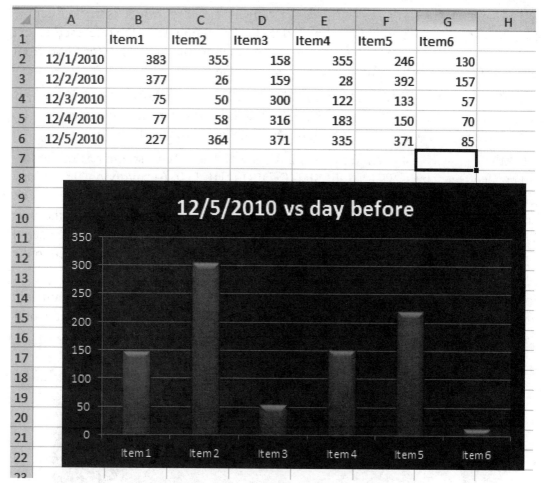

Figure 345

K	L	M	N	O	P
$F$6	FALSE	No Chart			
#N/A	#N/A	#N/A	#N/A	#N/A	#N/A

Figure 346

K	L	M	N	O	P	
$G$6	TRUE	12/5/2010 vs day before				
150	306	55	152	221	15	

Figure 347

What accounts for the difference? Notice cell K1. Its formula is =CELL("Address"). The syntax for the CELL function is =CELL(info_type,[reference]). If the reference is omitted, then the info type returned is based on the address of the active cell when the sheet was last calculated. So in Figure 344, the last cell changed(calculated) was F6, and in Figure 345, it was G6,

Cell L1 contains the formula =COLUMN(INDIRECT(K1))=7 which is true only if the last cell changed was in column G. The INDIRECT function treats the reference as text but converts it back to a reference. That is, K1 contains the *text* $G$6 (or $F$6 from Figure 345), so the indirect of this is the *reference* G6.

Cell M1 contains =IF(L1,TEXT(OFFSET(INDIRECT(K1),0,-6),"m/d/yyyy")&" vs day before","No Chart"). This says that if you didn't just enter the value in column G, then L1 would be FALSE, so this would return the text "No Chart".

But if the data was just entered in column G, then L1 is TRUE, so the rest of the formula is in effect. This is TEXT(OFFSET(INDIRECT(K1),0,-6),"m/d/yyyy")&" vs day before". Examine this further. INDIRECT(K1) is INDIRECT("$G$6") which is G6. So the OFFSET becomes OFFSET(G6,0,-6), which is A6, which contains the date 12/5/2010. Without enclosing this inside the TEXT function, you would see the serial #, or 40517, so this is just for formatting. The text " vs day before" is appended to the date.

How do you get the result of cell M1 as the title? Click on the title to select it, click in the formula bar, and type =Sheet2!$M$1. The chart title is picked up from the worksheet cell, and the chart title looks like this:

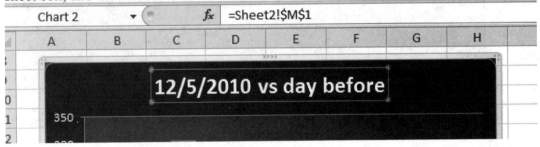

Figure 348

The rest of the data is picked up from K2:P2 and the chart is based on that. K2 contains a similar formula to the chart title:

=IF($L$1,OFFSET(INDIRECT($K$1),0,COLUMN(A1)-6)
-OFFSET(INDIRECT($K$1),-1,COLUMN(A1)-6),NA())

If L1 is FALSE, this will show #N/A, as seen in Figure 346. But if it's TRUE, then again the reference is to the INDIRECT(K1), and the calculation is OFFSET(INDIRECT($K$1),0,COLUMN(A1)-6) minus OFFSET(INDIRECT($K$1),-1,COLUMN(A1)-6) (the only difference being the row reference is 0 vs -1 so it subtracts the previous row from the current row . COLUMN(A1)-6 is -5, so in cell K2, this formula is effectively OFFSET(G6,0,-5) – OFFSET(G6,-1,-5) which is B6-B5, or 150, which is the value of the first column seen in Figure 345. Everything else in the formula is so that a simple fill right can be done, leaving the formula in P2 being: =IF($L$1,OFFSET(INDIRECT($K$1),0,COLUMN(F1)-6)-OFFSET(INDIRECT($K$1),-1,COLUMN(F1)-6),NA()).

The category axis labels came from editing the SERIES formula (note the reference to B1:G1) – to see it, simply click on any of the columns in the chart:

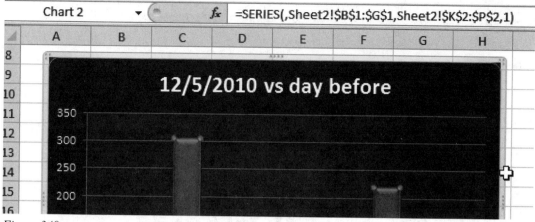

Figure 349

There are a lot of "features" used in this example:

- CELL("Address") – to get the address of the last cell entered
- INDIRECT – to change text to a reference
- OFFSET – to pick up values based on the location of the last cell entered
- COLUMN – for being able to fill right
- Editing the SERIES formula
- TEXT function to format a serial #

New to charting? Easiest way to get started is select ONE cell (or *all* cells) in the range you want to make a chart from, and press Alt+F1. That would give you the default of this:

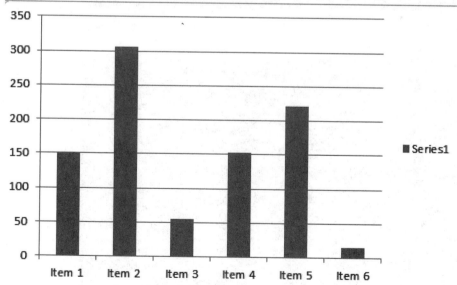

Figure 350

In the Design tab of the Chart contextual tabs, select style 44 from the gallery:

Figure 351

Then click on the legend and press the Delete key:

Figure 352

to get the chart shown here:

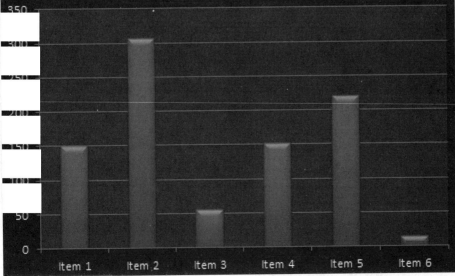

Figure 353

CHAPTER 7 - VBA

35-Ensure a Cell Contains a Value Before Saving File

Suppose you need to make sure a certain cell is not empty before the file is saved. For this example, Assume cell B3 must contain a value. You want this to happen if you try to save the file:

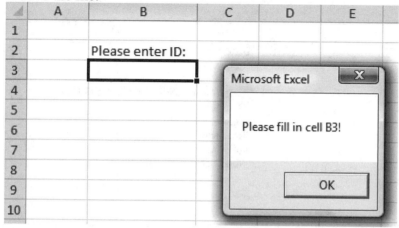

Figure 354

This requires fairly simple VBA code. Get to the VBE (Alt+F11), display the Project Explorer (Ctrl+R) and double-click the "ThisWorkbook" as shown in Figure 355, or right-click ThisWorkbook and select View Code as shown in Figure 356:

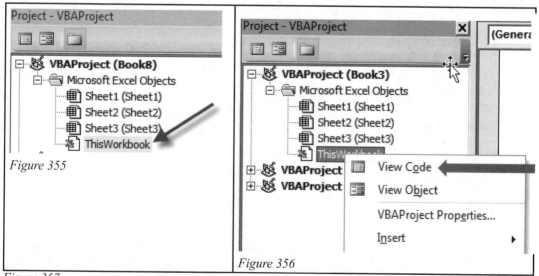

Figure 355

Figure 356

Figure 357

Select "Workbook" from the dropdown on the left:

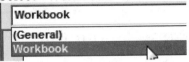

Workbook
(General)
Workbook

Figure 358

Then select BeforeSave in the right dropdown (you will probably have to scroll up to see this choice):

Workbook ▼	Open
Private Sub Workbook_Open() End Sub	AfterXmlImport BeforeClose BeforePrint BeforeSave ⬅ BeforeXmlExport BeforeXmlImport Deactivate NewChart NewSheet

Figure 359

And you'll see:

```
Workbook                              ▼   BeforeSave

   Private Sub Workbook_BeforeSave(ByVal SaveAsUI As Boolean, Cancel As Boolean)
       I

   End Sub
```

Figure 360

Inside this code you can type what you see here:

```
Private Sub Workbook_BeforeSave(ByVal SaveAsUI As Boolean, Cancel As Boolean)
    Cancel = (Len(ThisWorkbook.Sheets("Sheet1").Range("B3").Value) = 0)
    If Cancel Then
        ThisWorkbook.Activate 'in case another is active
        Sheets("Sheet1").Select
        Range("B3").Select
        MsgBox "Please fill in cell B3!"
    End If
End Sub
```

Figure 361

"Cancel" is a built-in parameter for the BeforeSave event. When it's true, the save will *not* be performed. It is set to the truth of Sheet1's cell B3 having a length of zero. That is, if the length is zero, the phrase

```
(Len(ThisWorkbook.Sheets("Sheet1").Range("B3").Value) = 0)
```

Figure 362

will be true, so the Cancel will be true. Then it's also tested to see if it's appropriate to give the message to the person.

36-A VBA User-Defined Function for Getting Sums from a Text String

Look at this figure:

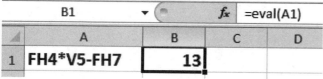

Figure 363

In this example, a reader had asked the author to take out the numbers only from a text string consisting of specifically FH or V preceding each number, then to perform the math indicated. For example, FH4*V5-FH7 would be interpreted as 4*5-7 (ignoring the FH & V), and yielding 13. If someone had entered FH3+FH9-V8, then the answer would be 3+9-8, or 4. Here, you'll examine a user-defined function to extract the numbers and perform the indicated arithmetic.

(UDF means User-Defined Function, by the way!)

In case this is your first foray into VBA, I'll take a step-by-step approach. First, to get to the VBE (Visual basic Environment), press Alt+F11, display the Project Explorer with Ctrl+R, then use Insert/Module:

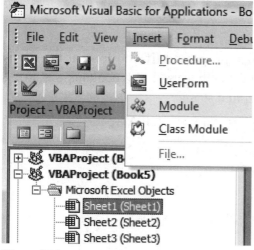

Figure 364

A Module is a place where the code is written. You will then see a blank area in which you write your code:

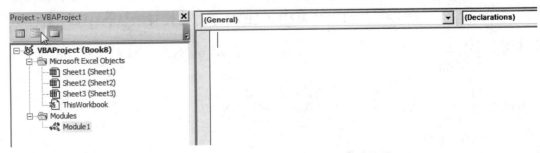

Figure 365

User-defined functions require the word Function, the name of the function, and, in this case, a parameter, or argument, containing the name which will hold the data passed from the spreadsheet. This will get clearer as you continue to read the example. In this case the function is called Eval (You could have named it practically anything).

Note that in the figures, the VBA editor format has been changed to use Comic Sans font, with keywords in red.

(General)

```
Function eval(Information)


End Function
```

Figure 366

The word Information will contain the information passed. If you look at the original figure in this example, you see =Eval(A1) is being used. A1 contains the string FH4*V5-FH7, so Information will also contain that string.

You are now going to work with "Information" as if it were cell A1.

(General)

```
Function eval(Information)
Dim Temp As String
    Temp = Replace(Information, "FH", "")
End Function
```

Figure 367

So now, if Information is FH4*V5-FH7, Temp is now 4*V5-7. (Temp is simply a name used to hold the value. You could just as well said Herman= Replace… or x=Replace… or gggsssshhh=Replace…, etc.)

Now you have to remove the "V":

```
Function eval(Information)
Dim Temp As String
    Temp = Replace(Information, "FH", "")
    Temp = Replace(Temp, "V", "")
End Function
|
```

Figure 368

Notice the use of the new value of Temp in the second line to strip the V. Temp is now 4*5-7.

In VBA there's a builtin function called Evaluate, and you can pass this new string to it. To return that value to the worksheet, you need to use the function name (Eval) as the result:

```
Function eval(Information)
Dim Temp As String
    Temp = Replace(Information, "FH", "")
    Temp = Replace(Temp, "V", "")
    eval = evaluaate(Temp)
End Function
```

Figure 369

Now it works fine:

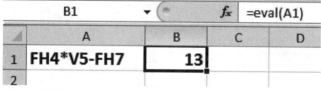

Figure 370

37-Delete Defined Names in One VBA Statement

As you can see in this figure, there are many defined names in this workbook:

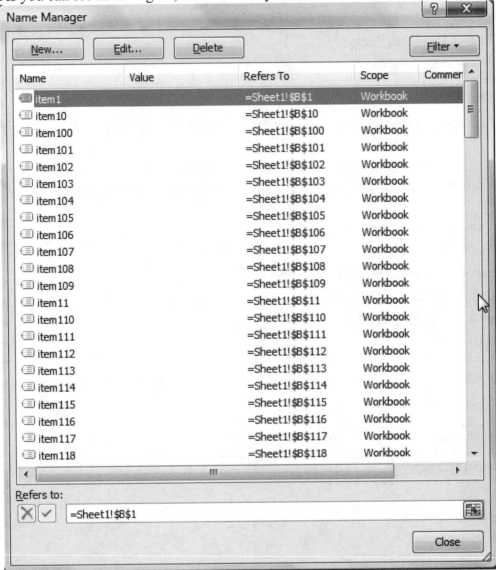

Figure 371

Deleting all of them manually is fairly easy – select them all and click the Delete button. You can select them all by scrolling to the bottom and holding the Shift key while clicking on the last name:

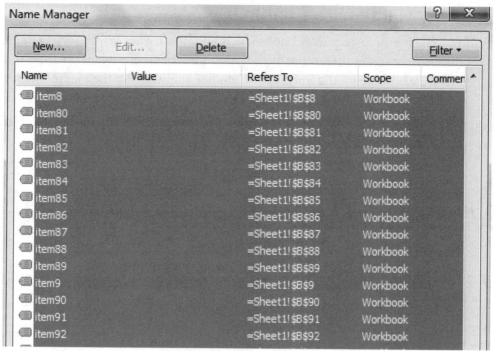

Figure 372

But to do it using VBA, most people would use a routine something like this (which works fine):

```
Sub DeleteAllNames()
    For Each nm In ActiveWorkbook.Names
        nm.Delete
    Next
End Sub
```

Figure 373

But here's the one-liner to do the same thing:

```
Sub DeleteAllNames()
    ExecuteExcel4Macro "Sum(Delete.name(names()))"
End Sub
```

Figure 374

This is a leftover from the Excel4 macro days, and the Excel4 macro statement =DE-LETE.NAME("xyz") would delete the name "xyz", and the statement =SUM(DELETE.NAME(NAMES())) was an array-entered statement in an Excel4 Macro sheet and still functions well in VBA as shown above.

38-Ensuring Macros are Enabled

There are times when you have a workbook which you don't want your users to open without having the macros in effect, but if they don't enable them when opening the workbook, or if they hold down the Shift key when opening the file, the macros won't run. Here's a way to make that useless for the person trying to bypass your macros.

First, if the user has his Macro settings to Enable All Macros Without Notification but holds down the shift key, they'd see this:

Macros must be enabled
in order to use this
workbook!

Figure 375

If they have the macro setting to disable all macros with notification, they'd see:

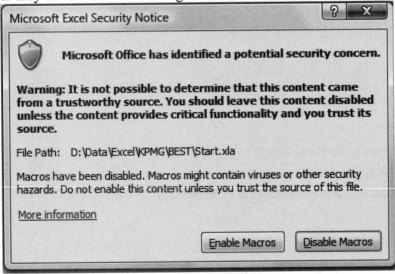

Figure 376

If they click Disable Macros they'd see the same as previously, and if they click Enable Macros, then of course, your macros run.

With the only sheet showing being Sheet1, the other sheets are all hidden from the user by the xlSheetVeryHidden property so it doesn't show in the Hide/Unhide. The code to give the user access to the normal workings of your workbook is here:

```
Workbook                              ▼    Open

    Private Sub Workbook_Open()
        ThisWorkbook.Unprotect "abc"
        For Each sh In Sheets
          sh.Visible = xlSheetVisible
        Next
        Sheet1.Visible = xlSheetVeryHidden
        ThisWorkbook.Windows(1).WindowState = xlMaximized
    End Sub
    Private Sub Workbook_BeforeClose(Cancel As Boolean)
        Sheet1.Visible = xlSheetVisible
        For Each sh In Sheets
          If sh.Name <> Sheet1.Name Then sh.Visible = xlSheetVeryHidden
        Next
        ThisWorkbook.Windows(1).WindowState = xlNormal
        ThisWorkbook.Protect "abc", True, True
    End Sub
```

Figure 377

In the Workbook_Open event (which won't run without macros enabled), the workbook is unprotected (of course, use a stronger password than "abc"!), then every sheet is made visible and the "splash" sheet is hidden, when the window is maximized.

Before the workbook is closed, the reverse is done. It makes the splash sheet (the one with the message) visible, hides every other sheet (with xlsheetVeryHidden), then restores the sheet to its small size, protects the workbook structure and windows, and saves the workbook.

The VBA code is also password protected – in the VBE, Tools/VBAProject Properties:

```
Tools  Add-Ins  Window  Help
   References...
   Additional Controls...
   Macros...
   Options...
   VBAProject Properties...
   Digital Signature...
```

Figure 378

Then choose Lock Project For Viewing and enter a password twice.

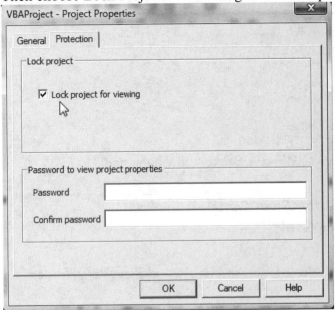

Figure 379

39-Getting a List of Sheet Tabs in a "Table of Contents"

Here's a pretty simple way, using VBA, to get a list of the tab names in the first sheet.

Here's the result, first:

	A	B	C	D	E	F
	A1			fx	=tabname(ROW(A1))	
1	Sheet1					
2	Sheet2					
3	Bob's Sheet					
4	Database					
5	Accounts					
6	Last Sheet					
7						

Figure 380

As you can see, a simple formula referencing a user-defined function called TabName and using ROW(A1) which in cell A1 returns 1, so this is TabName(1), and in A2 is TabName(ROW(A2)) which is TabName(2), and so on. To get TabName to work, you press Alt+F11, use Insert/Module, and enter this little piece of VBA code:

```
Function TabName(Ndx as Integer) As String
    On Error Resume Next  'In case parameter invalid.
    TabName = Sheets(Ndx).Name
End Function
```

Ndx, a made up name, is an integer value which references which Sheet you want to refer to. From cell A1, this evaluates to Ndx being a 1, and Sheets(1).Name is what's being assigned to the Function TabName.

40-Inserting Totals with VBA

Look at this figure:

◢	A	B	C	D
1	Bob	3/12/2010	$5,203	
2	Bob	4/7/2010	$5,186	
3	Bob	4/14/2010	$516	
4				
5				
6				
7	George	2/14/2010	$4,797	
8	George	3/30/2010	$5,544	
9	George	4/2/2010	$8,419	
10	George	4/26/2010	$3,863	
11				
12				
13	Jim	3/19/2010	Note1	$2,237
14	Jim	5/28/2010	Note2	$8,931
15				
16				
17				
18	Alicia	2/6/2010	$6,016	
19	Alicia	2/12/2010	$1,571	
20	Alicia	6/6/2010	$5,797	
21	Alicia	6/8/2010	$7,278	
22				

Figure 381

Not a good design, but this is what you have been given. Let's assume it goes on like this for hundreds of rows. Your task: put the total of each section in the first available space.

It doesn't look easy, especially with the section in rows 13:14 – the values are in a different column. So you must assume they may even be in still another column, like E or F, further down the page. You are about to see this done *with one line of code* inside a loop (so 3 lines including the For/Next lines). It executes lightning fast.

Before looking at the code, the thing is to take advantage of is the structure. If you did a GoTo Special and chose constants, it would look like this:

	A	B	C	D
1	Bob	3/12/2010	$5,203	
2	Bob	4/7/2010	$5,186	
3	Bob	4/14/2010	$516	
4				
5				
6				
7	George	2/14/2010	$4,797	
8	George	3/30/2010	$6,544	
9	George	4/2/2010	$8,419	
10	George	4/26/2010	$3,863	
11				
12				
13	Jim	3/19/2010	Note1	$2,237
14	Jim	5/28/2010	Note2	$8,931
15				
16				
17				
18	Alicia	2/6/2010	$6,016	
19	Alicia	2/12/2010	$1,571	
20	Alicia	6/6/2010	$5,797	
21	Alicia	6/8/2010	$7,278	

Figure 382

Excel can recognize these areas, and you'll want to take advantage of this. Use the same GoTo Special to work on each section.

Examine the code here:

```
Sub PutInTotals()
    For Each chunk In Cells.SpecialCells(xlCellTypeConstants).Areas
        chunk.Offset(chunk.Rows.Count, chunk.Columns.Count - 1).Resize(1, 1). _
            FormulaR1C1 = "=sum(r" & chunk.Row & "c:r[-1]c)"
    Next
End Sub
```

Figure 383

The one line mentioned is broken into two only because of the break character " _ " at the end of the line – it's really one line.

The loop starts with this:

For Each chunk In Cells.SpecialCells(xlCellTypeConstants).Areas

Figure 384

Cells refers to *all* the cells in the worksheet. SpecialCells is one of the GoTo Special choices – when you type part of it in the VBE, you're presented with a dropdown of choices:

cells.SpecialCells(

SpecialCells(***Type As XlCellType***, [*Value*]) As Range
▣ xlCellTypeAllValidation
▣ xlCellTypeBlanks
▣ xlCellTypeComments
▣ xlCellTypeConstants
▣ xlCellTypeFormulas
▣ xlCellTypeLastCell

Figure 385

Here, you pick xlCellTypeConstants which is all the cells containing constant values, whether numbers or text. One key thing you are looking at here is the end: ".Areas" – in the figure shown in this example, there are clearly four areas (of what you can see), and you are going to refer to one of those areas each time through the loop. The reference is called "chunk" – not a keyword. X could just as easily have used:

For Each x In Cells.SpecialCells(xlCellTypeConstants).Areas

Figure 386

The first time through the loop, "chunk" refers to A1:C3. Chunk.Offset(chunk.rows. count,chunk.columns.count-1) is key. Chunk.rows.count is 3, and chunk.columns. count is 3. So Chunk.Offset(3,3-1) is Chunk.Offset(3,2) which is C4:F6. If you did this:

Figure 387

then you'd see this:

▲	A	B	C	D	E
1	Bob	3/12/2010	$5,203		
2	Bob	4/7/2010	$5,186		
3	Bob	4/14/2010	$516		
4					
5					
6					
7	George	2/14/2010	$4,797		
8	George	3/30/2010	$6,544		

Figure 388

This is resized by 1 row & 1 column, so that's just cell C4. This is the cell to put the total in. This total should be the sum of the values from the first row of the section to the row above the cell containing the sum, and this does it:

[`"=sum(r" & chunk.Row & "c:r[-1]c)"`

Figure 389

Chunk.row is 1 in this case, so the formula is =SUM(r1c:r[-1]c) which in R1C1 notation for row 1 in the same column through the cell above in the same column.

One more (shorter) analysis for the third time through the loop, rows 13:14:

Now, "chunk" refers to A13:D13. Chunk.rows.count is 2, chunk.columns.count is 4, so Chunk.Offset(2,4-1) is Chunk.Offset(2,3), which is D15:G16 which you can verify by trying this:

Figure 390

When resized by 1,1 is simply cell D15, where you want the total. Final result:

	C4	▼	fx	=SUM(C$1:C3)

	A	B	C	D	
1	Bob	3/12/2010	$5,203		
2	Bob	4/7/2010	$5,186		
3	Bob	4/14/2010	$516		
4			$10,905		
5					
6					
7	George	2/14/2010	$4,797		
8	George	3/30/2010	$6,544		
9	George	4/2/2010	$8,419		
10	George	4/26/2010	$3,863		
11			$23,623		
12					
13	Jim	3/19/2010	Note1	$2,237	
14	Jim	5/28/2010	Note2	$8,931	
15				$11,168	
16					
17					
18	Alicia	2/6/2010	$6,016		
19	Alicia	2/12/2010	$1,571		
20	Alicia	6/6/2010	$5,797		
21	Alicia	6/8/2010	$7,278		
22			$20,662		
23					

Figure 391

41-Limiting Cells a Person Can Select Without Protecting the Worksheet

Suppose you wanted to limit the range a person could type to cells D3:H12. It can be done without VBA and without protection, but it does require a visit to the VBE (Visual Basic Environment). Simply right-click the sheet tab, select View Code, type D3:H12 in the ScrollArea property of the Properties window (if that's not visible, press F4) :

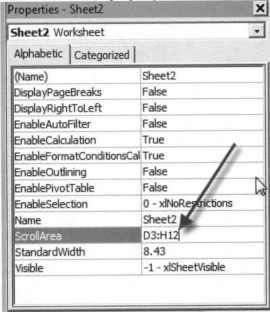

Figure 392

That's all there is to it! You can *see* outside the ScrollArea, but you can only select the cells in the range D3:H12.

This does not persist however if you close and re-open the Workbook. If you want it to be a permanent feature then you would need to put some VBA code in the Work-book_Open Event:

Private Sub Workbook_Open()

Sheets("Sheet1").ScrollArea = "D3:H12"

End Sub

If you need to cancel this then just set the ScrollArea Property to null:

Sheets("Sheet1").ScrollArea = ""

42-Many Buttons, One VBA Procedure

Look at Figure 393:

	A	B
1	10-digits.xlsx	Open
2	1234567.xls	Open
3	20 cdr.xlsx	Open
4	2008.501.xls	Open
5	2009 ONSITE AND PUBLIC SALES New Report.xls	Open
6	80000 Payment Summary.xls	Open
7	A&I - Falls Tracking Form 10-09.xls	Open
8	A04 - Timberlake Stock Cabinets - Inventory Magic 2008 v 2.xls	Open
9	AA.xls	Open
10	ACCU_EarlyLeads_-for_the_expeerts.xlsx	Open
11	AM102357001033.xlsx	Open
12	AMBO Week 13 '09-'10.xls	Open
13	AMB_Template.xlsm	Open
14	Amy-Vallidated_Mar2008_Text.xls	Open

Figure 393

A reader set up this workbook and asked if he really needed a procedure for each button (these are *form* buttons, not *ActiveX* buttons). This workbook went to row 230 or so! In fact, there's very little VBA code needed and it's all in the same procedure. Select *all* the buttons and assign one macro to them. You can select them all by Go To Special, Objects, or you can click on one of the buttons (if it hasn't yet been assigned to a macro) and then press Ctrl+Shift+Spacebar.

	A	B
1	10-digits.xlsx	Open
2	1234567.xls	Open
3	20 cdr.xlsx	Open
4	2008.501.xls	Open
5	2009 ONSITE AND PUBLIC SALES New Report.xls	Open
6	80000 Payment Summary.xls	Open
7	A&I - Falls Tracking Form 10-09.xls	Open
8	A04 - Timberlake Stock Cabinets - Inventory Magic 2008 v 2.xls	Open

Figure 394

Right-click any of the buttons and assign macro:

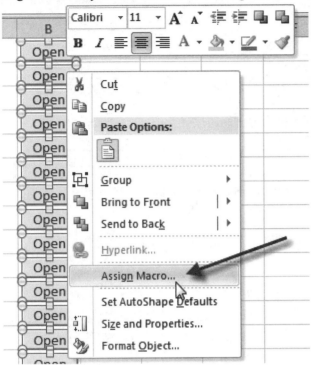

Figure 395

Make up a name, like OpenIt:

Figure 396

Now look at the OpenIt macro:

```
Sub OpenIt()
Dim RowOfButton As Long
    RowOfButton = ActiveSheet.Buttons(Application.Caller).TopLeftCell.Row
    Workbooks.Open Cells(RowOfButton, 1).Value
End Sub
```

Figure 397

Yes, that's all there is to it. How does it work? Application.Caller is the name of the object which called in the procedure. If you were to put a breakpoint at the first line (you can do this easily by clicking in the margin to the left of the code):

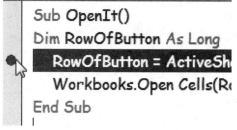

Figure 398

and click on any button (say the top one), then when you reach the breakpoint you can hover the mouse over Application.Caller and you see the name of the button which called in the procedure:

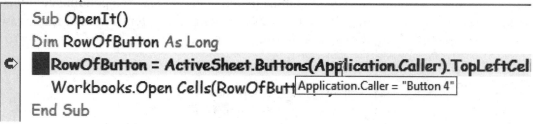

Figure 399

In this case. Activesheet.Buttons("Button 4") was the one which called it in. Objects have a TopLeftCell and BottomRightCell property. So the TopLeftCell's row is 1, so the value 1 is assigned to the variable called RowOfButton. Now, open the file (Workbooks.Open) in cell A1 because that's Cells(1,1).Value, or a file named "10-digits.xlsx" in this case.

43-Multiple Matches

Look at this worksheet:

	A	B	C	D	E	F
1						
2	item1	item2	item3	item4	item5	item6
3	item2	item3	item4	item5	item6	item1
4						
5						
6						
7						
8						
9						
10	item2	item8	item4	item9	item1	item10
11	item5	item7	item9	item1	item10	item3
12	item10	item6	item3	item5	item1	item4
13	item7	item2	item8	item4	item5	item10
14	item5	item4	item8	item7	item6	item9
15	item2	item5	item9	item7	item6	item10
16	item4	item5	item7	item8	item9	item10
17	item7	item3	item9	item4	item10	item6
18						

Figure 400

You want to be able to tell where there are at least three matches, if any, from rows 2 and 3, in rows 10 through 17. And they must match in the same corresponding columns. You can see them in this view. Notice that row 2 matches three items in row 13, and row 3 matches three items in row 15. The question is, how can you find them?

	A	B	C	D	E	F
1						
2	item1	item2	item3	item4	item5	item6
3	item2	item3	item4	item5	item6	item1
4						
5						
6						
7						
8						
9						
10	item2	item8	item4	item9	item1	item10
11	item5	item7	item9	item1	item10	item3
12	item10	item6	item3	item5	item1	item4
13	item7	item2	item8	item4	item5	item10
14	item5	item4	item8	item7	item6	item9
15	item2	item5	item9	item7	item6	item1
16	item4	item5	item7	item8	item9	item10
17	item7	item3	item9	item4	item10	item6
18						

Figure 401

This article will examine a formula approach initially taken to help create a user-defined function. I eventually discovered that there was a flaw in my thinking because the solution I'm about to propose doesn't work if cell A13 (or similar) contains a duplicate "item2". But I'm presenting it anyway because the approach is an interesting analysis and demonstrates some interesting ideas. And it *does* work if there are no duplicates!

First, look at how a formula could return a 3 (number of matches), when comparing row 2 with row 13:

| f_x | {=SUM(IFERROR(IF(COLUMN(A:F)=MATCH(A2:F2,A13:F13,0),1,0),0))} |

D	E	F	G	H	I	J
tem4	item5	item6		3		
tem5	item6	item1				

Figure 402

You see it's an array-entered formula, and it returns 3, the number of matches. Examine it a bit more closely. The MATCH part:

=SUM(IFERROR(IF(COLUMN(A:F)=MATCH(A2:F2,A13:F13,0),1,0),0))

Figure 403

when expanded by F9, shows:

=SUM(IFERROR(IF(COLUMN(A:F)={#N/A,2,#N/A,4,5,#N/A},1,0),0))

Figure 404

The first #N/A means A2 does not exist in range A13:F13. The 2 indicates item2 is found in the second position of A13:F13, and so on. If you take a quick look at how this would work using row 10, you would see:

=SUM(IFERROR(IF(COLUMN(A:F)={5,1,#N/A,3,#N/A,#N/A},1,0),0))

Figure 405

where the 5 shows item1 in the fifth position of A10:F10, etc. But you are looking for positional matches, which is this array is being compared to COLUMN(A:F).

The expansion of Figure 406 is Figure 407 because it compares Figure 408 respectively.

=SUM(IFERROR(IF(COLUMN(A:F)=MATCH(A2:F2,A13:F13,0),1,0),0))

Figure 406

=SUM(IFERROR(IF({#N/A,TRUE,#N/A,TRUE,TRUE,#N/A},1,0),0))

Figure 407

=SUM(IFERROR(IF({1,2,3,4,5,6}={#N/A,2,#N/A,4,5,#N/A},1,0),0))

Figure 408

You can see the TRUE values where the values correspond.

I want to digress for a moment to explain why you are using COLUMN(A:F) to get the values 1 through 6 instead of ROW(1:6) which also produces the values 1 through 6. The MATCH formula I'm using is against a horizontal range (notice the commas between the expanded values), so in order to get a useful comparison I also need a horizontal comparison, hence COLUMN(A:F). Had I used ROW(1:6), I would have come across 36 comparisons instead of the 6 I want! Look at this:

`=ROW(1:6)=COLUMN(A:F)`

Figure 409

When expanded, this gives this, which is 36 values instead of 6. Not good.

`={TRUE,FALSE,FALSE,FALSE,FALSE,FALSE;FALSE,TRUE,FALSE,FALSE,FALSE,FALSE;FALSE,FALSE,TRUE,FALSE,FALSE,FALSE;FALSE,FALSE,FALSE,TRUE,FALSE,FALSE;FALSE,FALSE,FALSE,FALSE,TRUE,FALSE;FALSE,FALSE,FALSE,FALSE,FALSE,TRUE}`

Figure 410

Okay, now back to the place before the digression!

This is inside an IF statement, because you want to count the TRUE's:

`=SUM(IFERROR(IF(COLUMN(A:F)=MATCH(A2:F2,A13:F13,0),1,0),0))`

Figure 411

Figure 411 expands to this:

`=SUM(IFERROR({#N/A,1,#N/A,1,1,#N/A},0))`

Figure 412

and passing this to the IFERROR gives this:

`=SUM(IFERROR({#N/A,1,#N/A,1,1,#N/A},0))`

Figure 413

or this:

`=SUM({0,1,0,1,1,0})`

Figure 414

So where's the problem? This works only if you know which row to look at! What's *really* wanted is something like this (notice the A10:F17 reference).

`{=SUM(IFERROR(IF(COLUMN(A:F)=MATCH(A2:F2,A10:F17,0),1,0),0))}`

D	E	F	G	H	I	J
n4	item5	item6		0		
n5	item6	item1				

Figure 415

Clearly that doesn't work. So a UDF comes in to play:

```
Function Mtch(SourceRow As Range, AnsRows As Range) As Integer
Dim ST1 As String, ST2 As String, ST3 As String
    ST1 = SourceRow.Address
    ST2 = AnsRows.Parent.Name
    Application.Volatile True
    For Each rw In AnsRows.Rows
        ST3 = rw.Address
        n = Evaluate("SUM(IFERROR(IF(COLUMN(A:F)=MATCH(" & ST1 & "," & ST2 & "!" & ST3 & ",0),1,0),0))")
        If n > 2 Then
            Mtch = rw.Row
            Exit Function
        End If
    Next
    Mtch = 0
End Function
```

Figure 416

As a side note, instead of using "As Integer", you can use "As Long" in case you're working with date which goes beyond row 32767! This UDF is called Mtch, and as you can see from the following, it returns the row number where there are at least three matches:

	A	B	C	D	E	F	G	H
						H2		=mtch(A2:F2,$A$10:$F$17)
1								
2	item1	item2	item3	item4	item5	item6		13
3	item2	item3	item4	item5	item6	item1		15
4								
5								
6								
7								
8								
9								
10	item2	item8	item4	item9	item1	item10		
11	item5	item7	item9	item1	item10	item3		
12	item10	item6	item3	item5	item1	item4		
13	item7	item2	item8	item4	item5	item10		
14	item5	item4	item8	item7	item6	item9		
15	item2	item5	item9	item7	item6	item1		
16	item4	item5	item7	item8	item9	item10		
17	item7	item3	item9	item4	item10	item6		

Figure 417

There are two parameters passed to this function: the row being checked, in cell H2 that's A2:F2, and the entire set of rows to compare, in this case A10:F17.

The function has three string variables, st1, st2, and st3. St1 is the address of the source row. For H2, that would come in as $A$2:$F$2. St2 is the name of the *sheet* containing the second range. This is so that the range which is now showing in A10:F17 could be on a different sheet, and the formula might be =mtch(A2:F2,Sheet2!$A$10:$F$17).

The line "Application.Volatile True" tells the function that it is to be recalculated whenever the worksheet is calculated.

The next key line is:

`For Each rw In AnsRows.Rows`

Figure 418

What's key is that AnsRows, which is A10:F17, is being scanned row by row and the variable rw represents one at a time. The first time through the loop, rw references A10:F10; the second time through the loop, rw is A11:F11, and so on.

String variable st3 is set to rw's address, so the first time, st3 is "$A$10:$F$10", etc.

The next key line is to create the same worksheet formula seen before, but in VBA, and evaluate its result. This is done by VBA's Evaluate function:

`n = Evaluate("SUM(IFERROR(IF(COLUMN(A:F)=MATCH(" & ST1 & "," & ST2 & "!" & ST3 & ",0),1,0),0))")`

Figure 419

It is built by putting the various strings together. The first time through the loop, st1 is A2:F2, st2 is A10:F10, and st3 is Sheet1, so this formula becomes

`SUM(IFERROR(IF(COLUMN(A:F)=MATCH($A$2:$F$2,Sheet1!$A$10:$F$10,0),1,0),0))`

Figure 420

Notice the single quotes are included in the building of the formula in case the referenced sheet contains blanks or special characters.

This formula is evaluated, as if it were entered into the spreadsheet, and held in variable n.

If n is greater than two (three or above), then the function name is set to the row number of rw and the function is exited. If not, the next row of A10:F17 is referenced by rw and the process continues. If it falls through without getting any matches over two, the function is set to zero.

There's another approach which is actually more accurate, since the above does NOT work when an item appears twice in a row, such as A13:B13:

	A	B	C	D	E	F	G	H	I	J
	H2				fx	{=SUM(IFERROR(IF(COLUMN(A:F)=MATCH(A2:F2,A13:F13,0),1,0),0))}				
1										
2	item1	item2	item3	item4	item5	item6		2		
3	item2	item3	item4	item5	item6	item1				
4										
5										
6						✛				
7										
8										
9										
10	item2	item3	item4	item5	item6	item1				
11	item5	item7	item9	item1	item10	item3				
12	item10	item6	item3	item5	item1	item4				
13	item2	item2	item2	item4	item5	item10				

Figure 421

These returned values, you remember, are the number of items which match, not the row numbers. Cell A13 has been changed to item2, and even though the shaded values between rows 2 and 13 still have three matches, the MATCH part of the formula becomes not usable. It evaluates to this:

=SUM(IFERROR(IF(COLUMN(A:F)={#N/A,1,#N/A,4,5,#N/A},1,0),0))

Figure 422

Initially that 1 was a 2, but now the item 2 is finding the field in column A, not column B. So the technique works if you can be sure the list of six items have no repeats!

What if they do? Then you can use the UDF on the following page instead. Since it's more universal, it's a better function, but I thought it useful to show the technique of applying a complicated worksheet formula inside VBA.

Look at the new approach.

```
Option Compare Text

Function Mtch(SourceRow As Range, AnsRows As Range) As Integer
    applicaiton.Volatile True
    For Each rw In AnsRows.Rows
        n = 0
        For i = 1 To 6
            If Application.Index(SourceRow, i) = Application.Index(rw, i) Then n = n + 1
        Next
        If n > 2 Then
            Mtch = rw.Row
            Exit Function
        End If
    Next
    Mtch = 0
End Function
```

Figure 423

For each of the 6 items in parameter SourceRow, you are comparing it to the corresponding value in rw. You can use the Application.Index of both SourceRow and rw to do this. Whenever there's a match, you can increment the counter n, which was set to 0 before the loop.

The Option Compare Text ensures a case-*in*sensitive comparison, or Item1 would not be equal to item1.

44-Overriding Cell Calculations

Often, in an application, you want to supply your user with the ability to override a cell's calculation, so you supply them with an override cell and a formula to accommodate this, as in this figure:

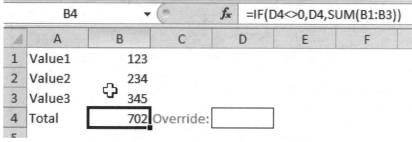

Figure 424

Here, the value in B4 is usually the sum of the cells above, but you supplied an override cell in D4, so it might become Figure 425:

B4			f_x	=IF(D4<>0,D4,SUM(B1:B3))	
	A	B	C	D	E	F
1	Value1	123				
2	Value2	234				
3	Value3	345				
4	Total	500	Override:	500		
5						

Figure 425

However, in an existing application, where you want to give the ability to override many cells, finding a good place to insert an override cell may be difficult. In this article Here is an interesting way to override cells.

Look at this figure:

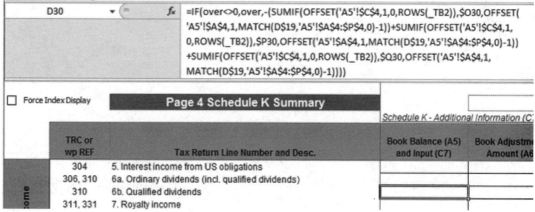

Figure 426

This is taken from a VERY large and complicated workbook (over 250 sheets and 50,000 lines of VBA code!) and with very complicated formulas (as in this example).

The "powers that be" wanted the ability to override most cells. The technique is not very complicated but has several pieces to it. For example, if one were to right-click on this cell, they'd see Figure 427.

Notice the "Override this cell…" at the bottom of the right-click menu. How this is determined is by the occurrence of the formula containing "over<>0". If a cell was selected which did not have a formula containing this text, then the Override this cell… would not show.

How *this* is accomplished is by this code in the Workbook_SheetBeforeRight-Click event shown below.

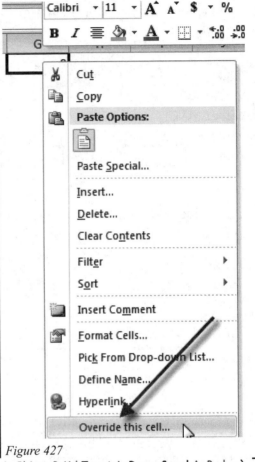

Figure 427

```
Private Sub Workbook_SheetBeforeRightClick(ByVal Sh As Object, ByVal Target As Range, Cancel As Boolean)
    With Application.CommandBars("Cell")
        On Error Resume Next
        .Controls("Override this cell...").Delete
        If InStr(Target.Formula, "over<>0") = 0 Then Exit Sub
        With .Controls.Add(msoControlButton)
            .Caption = "Override this cell..."
            .OnAction = "Override"
        End With
    End With
End Sub
```

Figure 428

First look at how *this* works. The right-click dropdown on a worksheet cell is referred to as Commandbars("Cell"). Inside event code, like above, you need to qualify this with "Application.".

There's an "On Error Resume Next" (third line) because it may be that the right-click does *not* have the control called "Override this cell…", and deleting it would create an error in the fourth line of this code. If the target's formula does not contain "over<>0", then you are done, so the Exit Sub is executed. The "Override this cell…" was already deleted, so it won't show.

If "over<>0" *is* found, then the caption "Override this cell…" is added, and the macro to run, "Override", is set up.

In each sheet which can contain this override feature, a section off to the right was set up and defined with a local name of "OverSection". This range is where all the overriding cells' values would be stored. Over is a range which is defined as a local name and a relative reference to many columns over. For example, in the initial worksheet shown, the definition of "over" is cell W30, that is, 19 cells to the right:

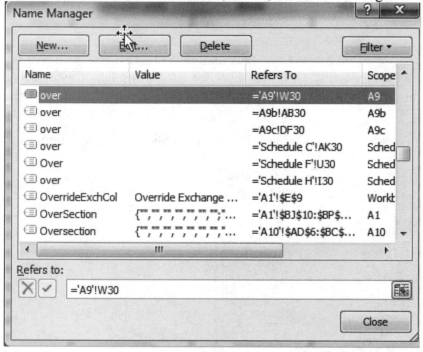

Figure 429

Notice it's a totally relative address – row *and* column. So another cell can use it's own "over" and reference a different cell. For example, here's D24's formula:

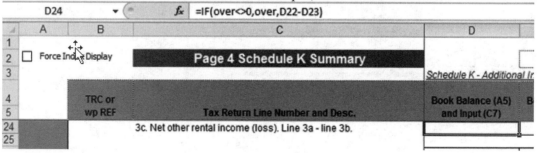

Figure 430

…"over" is cell W24 in this case.

The routine "Override" is seen here:

```
Sub OverRide()
    On Error Resume Next
    Dim Rg As Range
    Set Rg = Range("OverSection")
    If Err.Number <> 0 Then
        MsgBox "This sheet is not available for using the Override feature", vbExclamation, Ttl
        Exit Sub
    End If
    UFOverride.Show
End Sub
```

Figure 431

To ensure the applicability of the feature, the range named "OverSection" is tested for existence (this was set up manually on every sheet for which this feature was being used). It was done this way for ease in clearing all of the override cells at once, which you'll see shortly.

Basically, what this routine does is display a UserForm if all tests are satisfied. That form is seen here:

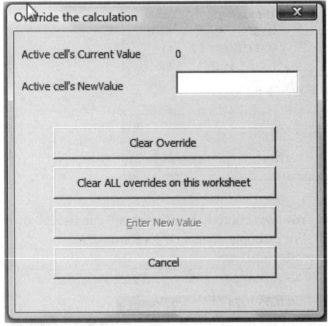

Figure 432

The code for each button will be displayed in a moment.

Next see what happens when the cell's value is overridden with this:

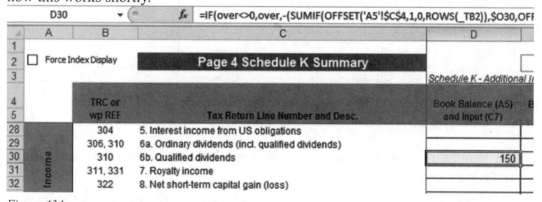

Figure 433

The result is shown here. It's yellow due to conditional formatting which you will see how this works shortly.

| D30 | | | f_x | =IF(over<>0,over,-(SUMIF(OFFSET('A5'!$C$4,1,0,ROWS(_TB2)),$O30,OFF |

	A	B	C	D
1				
2	☐ Force Index Display		Page 4 Schedule K Summary	☐
3				Schedule K - Additional I
4		TRC or		Book Balance (A5) B
5		wp REF	Tax Return Line Number and Desc.	and Input (C7)
28		304	5. Interest income from US obligations	
29		306, 310	6a. Ordinary dividends (incl. qualified dividends)	
30	Income	310	6b. Qualified dividends	150
31		311, 331	7. Royalty income	
32		322	8. Net short-term capital gain (loss)	

Figure 434

Cell W30 is seen in this figure:

| W30 | | | f_x | 150 |

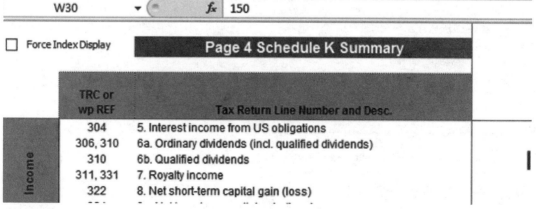

☐ Force Index Display   Page 4 Schedule K Summary

TRC or wp REF	Tax Return Line Number and Desc.
304	5. Interest income from US obligations
306, 310	6a. Ordinary dividends (incl. qualified dividends)
310	6b. Qualified dividends
311, 331	7. Royalty income
322	8. Net short-term capital gain (loss)

Figure 435

Notice the person never sees cell W30, and since the column is hidden, you can't tab to it.

The conditional formatting is pretty easy, too – all the cells which *may* get the override are selected as a block, and this is applied:

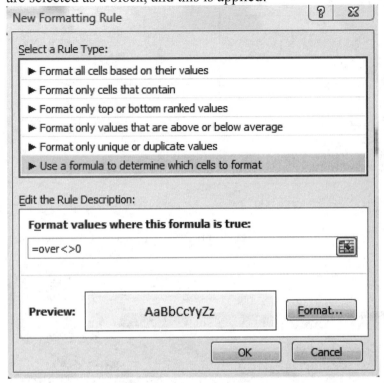

Figure 436

Simple formula of =over<>0. Since "over" is a relative reference to 19 cells to the right, it applies correctly to all the cells.

The only thing left to show is the other buttons on the UserForm. Here's the form in design mode:

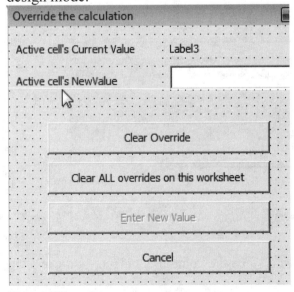

Figure 437

Here's the initialization code:

```
Private Sub UserForm_Initialize()
    If ActiveCell.Text = "" Then
        Me.Label3.Caption = "0"
    ElseIf IsError(ActiveCell.Value) Then
        Me.Label3.Caption = "0"
    Else
        Me.Label3.Caption = ActiveCell.Text
    End If
End Sub
```

Figure 438

This is all to change the Label 3 label. If the active cell is blank or an error, this field is zero, otherwise it's the current value as displayed in the cell.

The code for the Clear Override button also has an interesting quirk:

```
Private Sub CommandButton1_Click()
    Application.EnableEvents = False
    ActiveCell.Range("Over").ClearContents
    ActiveSheet.Calculate
    Application.EnableEvents = True
    Unload Me
End Sub
```

Figure 439

Notice the line ActiveCell.Range("Over").ClearContents. Why "ActiveCell."? Why not just Range("Over")? It's due to the nature of the relative reference. Look at this information in the immediate pane of the VBA:

```
Immediate
?range("over").Address
$T$1
?activecell.Range("over").Address
$W$1
```

Figure 440

Pretty unexpected! Range("Over") is assumed to be part of the worksheet collection, like Activesheet.Range("Over"), which has as its anchor point cell A1. 19 cells to the right of cell A1 is cell T1. But by using ActiveCell.Range("Over"), you are looking at 19 cells to the right of *the active cell*.

The code for the "Clear all overrides on this worksheet" is seen here:

```
Private Sub CommandButton4_Click()
    Application.EnableEvents = False
    Range("OverSection").ClearContents
    ActiveSheet.Calculate
    Application.EnableEvents = True
    Unload Me
End Sub
```

Figure 441

Now it's more obvious why the range called OverSection was created!

You may have noticed that the "Enter New Value" button is disabled. In creating the UserForm, the textbox was disabled as a property:

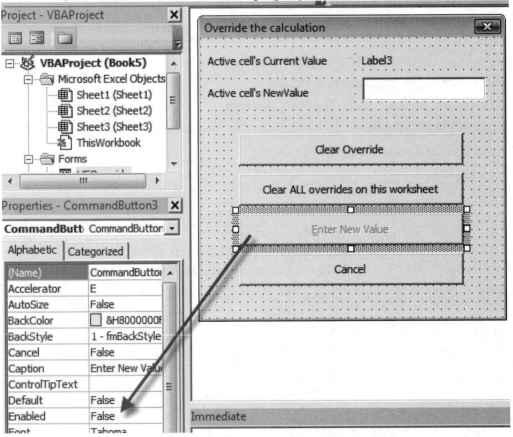

Figure 442

It gets enabled by the Change event of the new value's textbox. In design mode, double-clicking the textbox enables you to see (or enter) the code seen in Figure 443:

```
Private Sub TextBox1_Change()
  Dim ans As Double
  on error resumenext
  If Len(Me.TextBox1.Text) = 0 Then Exit Sub 'If the textbox is empty, keep the enabled state as False
  If Me.TextBox1.Text = "-" Then Exit Sub        'If the leading character is a -, there's more data to come, _
                                                  so leave the enabled state as False
    ans = 1 * Me.TextBox1.Text                    'Multiply by 1 to see if it's valid
  If Err.Number <> 0 Then 'Not valid
    MsgBox "Numeric values only, please", vbExclamation, Ttl
    Me.CommandButton3.Enabled = False
    Exit Sub
  End If
  'If we fall through to here, all is OK
  Me.CommandButton3.Enabled = True
End Sub
```

Figure 443

One last thing – you may think it's quite tedious to change all the existing formulas to *insert* the beginning of the formula to be =IF(over<>0,over,*currentformula*) but this can be handled by a utility macro like this – first select all the cells for which the overriding formulas need to be inserted, then run this code:

```
Sub EnterOver()
  For Each Thing In Selection
    If Thing.HasFormula Then
      Thing.Formula = "IF(over<>0,over," & Mid(Thing.Formula, 2) & ")" 'bypass the "=" sign
    End If
  Next
End Sub
```

Figure 444

To summarize the pieces needed to implement something like this:
- You need a definition of a local, relative-named cell which uses an area outside the current used area and for which all the columns are hidden and the contents are unprotected. Here, "over" was used as the local name – local so that it can be used on all sheets.
- The entire area comprising the override range is another locally named range, named OverSection (or any name you'd like to use).
- The cells which can be overridden are selected as a block and given a simple conditional format of =over<>0 so a user knows the calculation is not the usual one, but has been overridden.
- You need a UserForm to handle the clearing and setting of the overrides.
- You need code to handle the right-mouse click in which the formula is tested to see if it contains the text "over<>0"
- You need the code to bring up the UserForm.

45-Quick Way to Put Sequential Numbers into a Range Using VBA

How would you fill the range A1:A100 with the values 1 thru 100 using VBA? There are a number of approaches.

This first one loops through each cell in column A and places the value of the loop index, i, in the cell. It works, but is probably the slowest of these methods.

```
Sub NotSoQuick()
    For i = 1 To 100
        Cells(i, 1).Value = i
    Next
End Sub
```

Figure 445

This next one places the values 1 and 2 in cells A1:A2, then "uses" the Fill Handle to drag down to A100.

```
Sub Quick1()
    Range("A1").Value = 1
    Range("A2").Value = 2
    Range("A1:A2").AutoFill Destination:=Range("A1:A100"), Type:=xlFillDefault
End Sub
```

Figure 446

This one puts the formula =ROW() into each cell, then copies it and pastes values into the same cells.

```
Sub Quick2()
    With Range("A1:A100")
        .Formula = "=ROW()"
        .Copy
        .PasteSpecial xlPasteValues
    End With
End Sub
```

Figure 447

Here's a version which uses the Fill Series and is pretty quick as well:

```
Sub Quick2A()
    Range("A1").Value = 1
    Range("A1").DataSeries Rowcol:=xlColumns, Stop:=100
End Sub
```

These last two are probably the quickest, and the least intuitive. There's an Evaluate function in VBA which is somewhat like clicking in the Formula bar and highlighting the formula or part of it and pressing the F9 key. If you highlighted this:

```
=ROW(1:100)
```

Figure 448

and pressed F9, you'd see this:

```
={1;2;3;4;5;6;7;8;9;10;11;12;13;14;15;16;17;18;19;20;21;22;23;24;25;26;27;28;29;30;31;32;33;34;
35;36;37;38;39;40;41;42;43;44;45;46;47;48;49;50;51;52;53;54;55;56;57;58;59;60;61;62;63;64;65;
66;67;68;69;70;71;72;73;74;75;76;77;78;79;80;81;82;83;84;85;86;87;88;89;90;91;92;93;94;95;96;
97;98;99;100}
```

Figure 449

That's like using this routine:

```
Sub Quick3()
    Range("A1:A100") = Evaluate("row(1:100)")
End Sub
```

Figure 450

This next one is equivalent (the "[" and "]" symbols are pretty equivalent to Evaluate, but as you can see, the quotes are not necessary):

```
Sub Quick4()
    Range("A1:A100") = [row(1:100)]
End Sub
```

Figure 451

If you wanted to get something like 5, 10, 15, etc. into range A1:A100, you can similarly use this code:

```
Sub Quick5()
    Range("A1:A100") = [Row(1:100)*5]
End Sub
```

Figure 452

46-Trimming and Cleaning all Cells on a Worksheet

Thanks to Joe Sorrenti (a co-worker of the author) for this technique.

Many people import data from other sources. This data often needs to be cleansed by removing unprintable characters such as carriage returns and line feeds and leading and trailing spaces to be useful.

Most people would probably write a routine such as the one shown in Figure 453, which works fine:

```
Sub TrimAndClean()
    Dim Rng As Range
    For Each Rng In ActiveSheet.UsedRange.Cells
        Rng.Value = Replace(Application.Clean(Trim(Rng.Value)), Chr(160), "")
    Next
End Sub
```

Figure 453

The above method is fine for limited amounts of data. However, if there are many thousands of rows of data, it may take several minutes for the above code to run.

A more efficient method is to read each area of the worksheet into an array and process the array in memory and write the array back to the worksheet such as in the routine below. While it's a much longer procedure, it runs nearly instantly:

```
Sub TrimAndCleanAll()
    Dim r As Range, ar As Range
    Dim v, j As Long, k As Long
    Dim blnEvents As Boolean
    On Error GoTo ErrHandler
    blnEvents = Application.EnableEvents   'hold current state of events
    If blnEvents Then Application.EnableEvents = False 'turn events off
    Set r = ActiveSheet.UsedRange.SpecialCells(xlCellTypeConstants)
    For Each ar In r.Areas   'loop through each non-contiguous range on worksheet
        v = ar.Value   'read the area into an array
        If IsArray(v) Then 'area has multipls cells
            'now process the array in memory:
            For j = LBound(v, 1) To UBound(v, 1)        'if the range is F3:J12 then this is 1 to 10 (# rows)
                For k = LBound(v, 2) To UBound(v, 2)       'if the range is F3:J12 then this is 1 to 5 (# cols)
                    v(j, k) = Replace(Application.Clean(Trim(v(j, k))), Chr(160), "")
                Next
            Next
            ar.Value = v   'write the array back to the worksheet
        Else   'one cell in area
            ar.Value = Replace(Application.Clean(Trim(v)), Chr(160), "")
        End If
    Next
ExitHere:
    Application.EnableEvents = blnEvents   'restore events
    Exit Sub
ErrHandler:
    If Err.Number = 1004 And Err.Description Like "*No cells*" Then
        Resume ExitHere   'no cells on worksheet
    Else
        MsgBox "Error:" & Err.Number & vbCr & Err.Description
        Resume ExitHere
    End If
End Sub
```

Figure 454

47-Using a Demo of a File – Not Allowing it to be Used More than X Times

Suppose you want to send out a demo version of a file for a someone to examine, but you don't want it used more than a certain number of times, perhaps without your being paid for it. There are a lot of possible approaches for this situation, but here you will learn to use of some simple VBA statements called SaveSetting and GetSetting.

Here's a screenshot of the whole procedure. It's run each time the workbook is opened. If the VBA code is password protected the user will not be able to easily prevent the demo program from ending.

```
Private Sub Workbook_Open()
    n = GetSetting("Demo", "Demo", "Demo", 0) + 1
    If n > 5 Then
        MsgBox "This file has reached its maximum usage", vbCritical
        Application.Quit
    End If
    SaveSetting "Demo", "Demo", "Demo", n
End Sub
```

Figure 455

The syntax for GetSetting is shown here:

```
getsetting(
```

GetSetting(**AppName As String**, Section As String, Key As String, [Default]) As String

Figure 456

The syntax for SaveSetting is shown here:

```
savesetting(
```

SaveSetting(**AppName As String**, Section As String, Key As String, Setting As String)

Figure 457

Each of the parameters is an arbitrary name you supply to access information stored in or read from the registry.

The AppName is more like a major category, the Section is a subcategory and the Key is yet another category. It gets clearer with the example. The first time this workbook is opened, the statement

N=GetSetting("Demo","Demo","Demo",0)+1 is executed. The fourth parameter is the default value given if no setting is actually already stored. So the first time, the GetSetting returns 0. Adding 1 to this stores a 1 into variable n.

So n is *not* 5 (yet), and it runs into the SaveSetting. The statement SaveSetting "Demo", "Demo", "Demo", n now stores the value 5 in the registry. The next time the workbook is opened, the GetSetting returns that 1, and 1 is added to it and stored in n. Still not 5, and now a 2 is stored in the registry, etc. Eventually, the GetSetting returns 5, n is 6, and the program quits after giving a message to the user.

To reset this to zero on your own machine, you can either run SaveSetting "Demo", "Demo", "Demo", 0, or you can run another variation of the VBA, called DeleteSetting. This syntax is shown here:

```
deletesetting(
DeleteSetting(AppName As String, [Section], [Key])
```

Figure 458

As you can see the Section and Key are optional. So executing DeleteSetting "Demo" clears the registry of the AppName as well as Section and Key.

Using GetSetting, SaveSetting, DeleteSetting can enable you to also communicate between sessions of Excel, or one of my favorite ways to use it is in debugging. I have frequently come across some stumpers where the VBA code crashes and I'm unable to pinpoint where that happens. This is with over 40,000 lines of VBA code (yes, a *very* large and intricate set of macros!) The idea of single stepping through the code is good, but there are times when I do that, then the error doesn't occur! So I intersperse my code with random lines of something like SaveSetting "X", "X", "X", 1 and Save-Setting "X", "X", "X", 2 and SaveSetting "X", "X", "X", 3, etc, and once the program crashes I start up excel and run this line in the immediate window: ?GetSetting ("X", "X", "X") and if it returns 2, for example, then I know the program crashed between the SaveSetting which produced a 2 and the one which produced a 3. It has helped.

Lastly, the value stored is not limited to numbers as you've seen in this example – it can be any string you want, using it like a storage area for any purpose.

48-Using Excel Ranges With the VBA Join Method

Thanks to Joe Sorrenti (a co-worker of the author and technical editor) for this technique. Look at this figure:

	A	B	C	D	E	F
1	A	B	C	D	E	F
2						
3						
4						
5						
6	A					
7	B					
8	C					
9	D					
10	E					
11	F					

Figure 459

If you wanted to join the A thru F values to produce this:

	A	B	C	D	E	F	G
1	A	B	C	D	E	F	ABCDEF
2							
3							
4							
5							
6	A						
7	B						
8	C						
9	D						
10	E						
11	F						
12	ABCDEF						
13							

Figure 460

then you could would write a looping procedure to combine the values into G1 and A12 something like this procedure, which works fine:

```
Sub JoinCells1()
    Dim Rng As Range
    Dim strVal As String
    For Each Rng In Range("A1:F1")
        strVal = strVal & Rng.Value
    Next
    Range("G1").Value = strVal
    strVal = Empty
    For Each Rng In Range("A6:A11")
        strVal = strVal & Rng.Value
    Next
    Range("A12").Value = strVal
End Sub
```

Figure 461

However, there's another way. The VBA join method offers an interesting twist to solve this issue.

The JOIN Method accepts an array as an input. However, if a range is passed in as the array, a runtime error will occur. The trick is to use the Excel Transpose function on vertical ranges and the *double* transpose for the horizontal range of A1:F1.

```
Sub JoinCells2()
    With Application
        Range("A12").Value = Join(.Transpose(Range("A6:A11").Value), "")
        Range("G1").Value = Join(.Transpose(.Transpose(Range("A1:F1").Value)), "")
    End With
End Sub
```

Figure 462

CHAPTER 8 - MISCELLANEOUS

49-What Really is the Issue with Dates?

What does "one month away" really mean? Most of the time, it's pretty obvious. Clearly you can't just add 30 days or 31 days due to the varying number of days in a month. But trying to use something like =DATE(YEAR(A1),MONTH(A1)+1,DAY(A1)) often yields odd results. Why is this?

First, let's verify there's a problem:

C1			*fx*	=DATE(YEAR(A1),MONTH(A1)+1,DAY(A1))	
	A	B	C	D	E	F
1	5/5/2011		6/5/2011			
2						

Figure 463

This one looks fine. Let's have another look:

C1			*fx*	=DATE(YEAR(A1),MONTH(A1)+1,DAY(A1))	
	A	B	C	D	E	F
1	1/30/2011		3/2/2011			
2						

Figure 464

Whoa! Clearly something's not right! Why? Well, what *is* one month from January 30? February 30? No such thing. Look again:

C1			*fx*	=DATE(YEAR(A1),MONTH(A1)+1,DAY(A1))	
	A	B	C	D	E	F
1	2/2/2011		3/2/2011			
2						

Figure 465

Hey – if 1/30/2011 in A1 gives 3/2/2011 in C1 and 2/2/2011 in A1 gives 3/2/2011 in C1, then one can assume that 1/30/2011 is the same as 2/2/2011!

So you can see it's not really possible to define what a month really is in Excel. And this is also why it's not possible, given a person's birth date, to say how old he is described as x Years, y Months, and z Days. The only real definition is something like 48.918377723 years old!

By the way, DATE(YEAR(A1),MONTH(A1)+1,0) (note the 0 for the day) is one day before DATE(YEAR(A1),MONTH(A1)+1,1) which is the first day of a month, so the 0 is a way of getting the *last* day of a month!

50-Getting Sums From a Text String, Revisited

Look at this figure:

▲	A	B
1	FH4+V8	12
2	FH2+V12	14
3	FH11+V15	26

Figure 466

A reader from a newsgroup asked the author how to get the values shown in column B from the data in column A. That is, add the number parts, so cell A1 is 4+8, A2 is 2+12, and A3 is 11+15. FH stood for "Floating Holiday" and V for "Vacation". So the text was *always* FH & V followed by numbers. This is one solution I came up with. My first thought was that if I could simply get 4+8 in a cell, then maybe the VALUE function would work. I tried it:

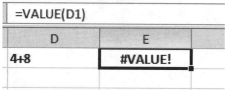

	D	E	
	4+8	#VALUE!	

Figure 467

Guess not! Then I remembered that there is an old Excel4 function called EVALUATE which still works as a defined name, so I tried that:

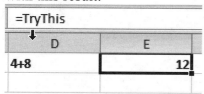

Figure 468

with this result:

=TryThis

	D	E
	4+8	12

Figure 469

Cool. So all I really needed to do was strip the FH and V and I have it. That can be done with a pair of SUBSTITUTE functions:

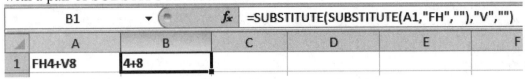

	A	B	C	D	E	F
1	FH4+V8	4+8				

Figure 470

So this solution is a defined name, FHV:

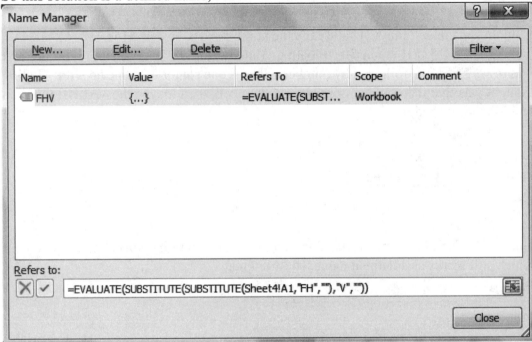

Figure 471

Cell B1 was selected when the name was defined (important), so I could use the "!A1" inside the definition as a relative reference to the cell to the left. Putting in the exclamation point, though not necessary here but included to show this extra tip, stops Excel from appending the sheet name to the reference, so it's valid on all sheets in the workbook.

So the initial screen shot, shown at the beginning of this example, with formulas showing is seen here:

	A	
1	FH4+V8	=FHV
2	FH2+V12	=FHV
3	FH11+V15	=FHV
4		

Figure 472

This works because each formula is the relative reference to the cell to the left. By the way, this would also work with other combinations of arithmetic operators. Here, you see 4 * 5 – 7 working out well:

	B1			f_x	=FHV	
	A	B	C			
1	FH4+V8	12				
2	FH2+V12	14				
3	FH11+V15	26				
4						

Figure 473

51-Useful Filtering Technique

Look at this figure:

	A	B	C	D	E	F
1	Date	Accounts	Description	Debit	Credit	0
2	1/1/2009	Cash	Against Invoice #1	50,000.00		50,000.00
3	1/1/2009	Capital	Against Invoice #1		50,000.00	-
4	1/2/2009	Purchases	Against Invoice #2	10,000.00		10,000.00
5	1/2/2009	Cash	Against Invoice #2		10,000.00	-
6	1/3/2009	Cash	Against Invoice #3	20,000.00		20,000.00
7	1/3/2009	Sales	Against Invoice #3		20,000.00	-
8						

Figure 474

The formula in cell F2 is filled in column F and represents the accumulated debits less credits. But see what happens here if you filter the Accounts on Cash only:

	A	B	C	D	E	F
1	Date	Accounts	Description	Debit	Credit	0
2	1/1/2009	Cash	Against Invoice #1	50,000.00		50,000.00
5	1/2/2009	Cash	Against Invoice #2		10,000.00	-
6	1/3/2009	Cash	Against Invoice #3	20,000.00		20,000.00
8						

Figure 475

Now the numbers don't really make sense. What's wanted is shown here:

	A	B	C	D	E	F
1	Date	Accounts	Description	Debit	Credit	0
2	1/1/2009	Cash	Against Invoice #1	50,000.00		50,000.00
5	1/2/2009	Cash	Against Invoice #2		10,000.00	40,000.00
6	1/3/2009	Cash	Against Invoice #3	20,000.00		60,000.00
8						

Figure 476

But what formula can accomplish this?

Y simply want the debits so far less the credits so far, just for the visible cells, and this is accomplished with the SUBTOTAL(109,...) formula:

	A	B	C	D	E	F
	F2		fx	=SUBTOTAL(109,$D$1:$D2)-SUBTOTAL(109,$E$1:$E2)		
1	Date	Accounts	Description	Debit	Credit	0
2	1/1/2009	Cash	Against Invoice #1	50,000.00		50,000.00
5	1/2/2009	Cash	Against Invoice #2		10,000.00	40,000.00
6	1/3/2009	Cash	Against Invoice #3	20,000.00		60,000.00
8						

Figure 477

Notice the references carefully in cell F2: The accumulated debits is =SUBTOTAL(109,$D$1:$D2) which adds the *visible* data from D1:D2. The same formula in F6 is shown here:

	A	B	C	D	E	F
	F6		fx	=SUBTOTAL(109,$D$1:$D6)-SUBTOTAL(109,$E$1:$E6)		
1	Date	Accounts	Description	Debit	Credit	0
2	1/1/2009	Cash	Against Invoice #1	50,000.00		50,000.00
5	1/2/2009	Cash	Against Invoice #2		10,000.00	40,000.00
6	1/3/2009	Cash	Against Invoice #3	20,000.00		60,000.00
8						

Figure 478

Of course, the accumulated visible credits are subtracted from the accumulated visible debits, which also has the reference go from row 1 through the current row.

52-Referencing in Long Worksheets

The challenge for this technique was that the worksheet had nearly 32000 rows, broken into 21 "sets" of 1523 rows. Each set had *one* key figure which determined if the entire set should be seen or not. The key rows had the formula as shown in Figure 479. Figure 480 simply shows the bottom of the worksheet.

Notice that B7 through B1529 contain the exact same formula, =IF(T513=0,1,NA()). This formula is used in code to determine if the row should be shown via this code in the worksheet_activate event:

```
Range("B7:B31987").EntireRow.Hidden = False
Range("B7:B31987").SpecialCells(xlCellTypeFormulas, _
    xlNumbers).EntireRow.Hidden = True
```

The above 2 VBA statements first unhide all the rows, then hide the rows which contain a number.

The next 1,523 rows contain a different formula, but they're all the same as well, namely =IF(T2036=0,1,NA()).

The problem was, how can these 32,000 formulas be entered? You can't simply fill them down because the T513 would become T514, T515, etc.

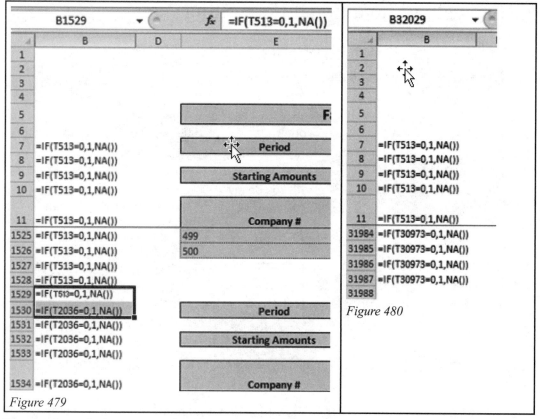

Figure 479

Figure 480

Here's the solution: – enter this in B7: =IF(T$513=0,1,NA()) and fill this to B1529. Since the absolute row reference was present, it remained 513 for all the cells. Then use Replace to change "$" to nothing. Then copy B7:B1529, selected B1530:B31987 and did a paste and all was perfect!

53-Interesting Conditional Formatting

Look at this figure:

	A	B	C	D	E
1	My vehicle is a truck	When in doubt, pass	this is a long book	This is a book	An apple a day
2	Imagine life before the internet	Play backgammon	I don't understand	I like riding on an airplane	keeps the doctor Away
3	Airplanes should have electric outlets	I gave a car	Will you be my valentine?	Excel is great!	Read a book
4	Do you like the dummies books?	Taxes are coming soon	That hurts	Motorcycles are cool	the time is now
5	Acknowledge someone today	Vans are fuel inefficient	Time for a vacation	So, what's new?	Home is where the heart is
6	Is this fie-tuned?	Advertise here	I learned how to ride a bicycle	Press Alt/7 on keypad for a bullet	Go Home

Figure 481

The cells which are highlighted are cells which contain any of the words listed:

K
car
truck
plane
Apple
motorcycle
bicycle
van

Figure 482

The conditional formatting formula is shown here:

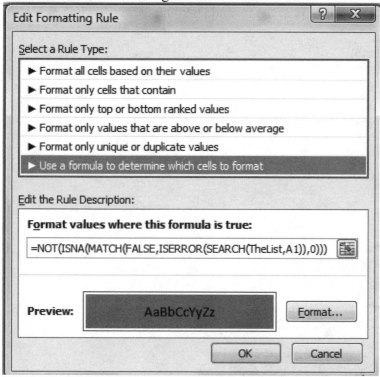

Figure 483

First, use a worksheet formula against one cell to get started:

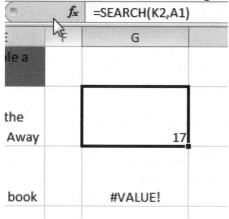

Figure 484

Cell G2 gives 17, the location of the word "truck" in cell A1 ("My vehicle is a truck"). Cell G2 was filled down to G3 – =SEARCH(K3,A2) which gives a #VALUE! error.

Now apply this to a *range* of cells, not just one cell. In Figure 485, you can see another #VALUE!, but if you select the formula in the formula bar and press F9, you see Figure 486.

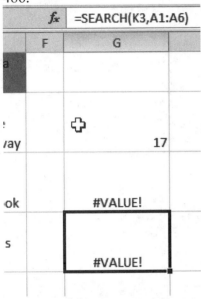

Figure 485

={#VALUE!;#VALUE!;4;#VALUE!;#VALUE!;#VALUE!}

Figure 486

Notice the "4" inside this string of results. That means there's a "hit"! If you pass this into an ISERROR function, you will have material to work with:

=ISERROR(SEARCH(K3,A1:A6))

Figure 487

expands to

={TRUE;TRUE;FALSE;TRUE;TRUE;TRUE}

Figure 488

See the "FALSE"? That's good! The existence of FALSE inside this formula means the word exists! So you can use MATCH to see if FALSE is present:

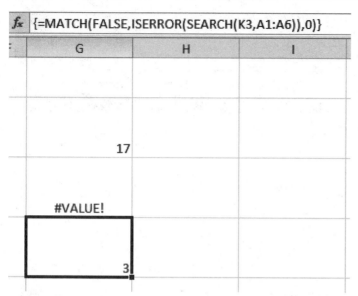

Figure 489

This becomes 3, since FALSE is in the third position. Notice it's array-entered because of the SEARCH(K3,A1:A6) part of the formula. What if it's *not* found? This would produce a #N/A error, That is,

```
{=ISNA(MATCH(FALSE,ISERROR(SEARCH(K3,A1:A6)),0))}
```

Figure 490

would give TRUE since K1 ("car") is not in any of the cells A1:A6. So when this function produces TRUE, it's *not* found. You will need to reverse that so you know when it *is* found, and the conditional formula becomes:

```
{=NOT(ISNA(MATCH(FALSE,ISERROR(SEARCH(K3,A1:A6)),0)))}
```

Figure 491

However you don't want to look for simply *one* value from column K, as you've been showing, but *all* the values. In this example, that would be

```
{=NOT(ISNA(MATCH(FALSE,ISERROR(SEARCH(K1:K6,A1:A6)),0)))}
```

Figure 492

Since the list in K can grow (or shrink), a defined name, "TheList" was used, which is seen in Figure 493:

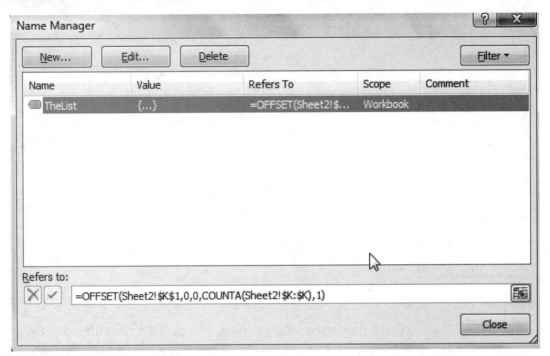

Figure 493

The range defines itself based on the number of items in column K. So the original range, A1:E6 was selected, and the formula you developed was applied. That formula is =NOT(ISNA(MATCH(FALSE,ISERROR(SEARCH(TheList,A1)),0))) and since it's being placed inside the conditional formatting form, there's no array-enter ability, so it assumes all formulas *are* array entered, and it works!

54-Highlighting Cells Which are Values Which Should Be Formulas, Without Using VBA

Suppose you have a workbook which looks like this:

	E5			f_x	=IF(ISERROR(A4AdjBook),0,A4AdjBook)	
	A	B	C		D	E
1						Provision/Book to Return Reconciliatio
2						
3						
4	Prior Year	Cons Code	CY wp REF	Description		Tax Return
5	1,809,454		A4	Net Book Income (Loss) from Trial Balance		(118,959,036)
6	66,597			Net Book Income (Loss) Override		
7	251,751		A6	Adjusting Journal Entries		(53,680)
8	318,348			Adjusted Net Book Income (Loss)		(119,012,716)
9	122,425	C	M4	m4		91,188
10	107,590	C	S6	State and Local Income Taxes		123,456,789
11	(181,947)	C	M6	m6		600
12	366,416			Net Book Income Before Tax		4,535,861

Figure 494

The worksheet isn't protected, so someone could type a value into the cells with formulas. This technique will show you how you can conditionally format cells which should be formulas but aren't, without using VBA.

One thing you need to be able to do is distinguish formulas from non-formulas. There's no built-in way to do this, but the old Excel4-style macro commands are still available. You are going to use GET.CELL(6,ref) which returns a text string formula of a cell. So for example, if you define the name "test" to be =GET.CELL(6,'A1'!$E$5) as seen here (the name of the sheet is A1, so Excel supplies single quotes around it):

New Name

Name: Test

Scope: Workbook

Comment:

Refers to: =get.cell(6,'A1'!$E$5)

OK   Cancel

Figure 495

and then enter =test in a cell, you see this:

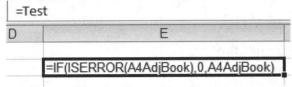

```
=Test
```

D	E
	=IF(ISERROR(A4AdjBook),0,A4AdjBook)

Figure 496

So if you use a relative reference in the GET.CELL for the active cell, then you can apply the name to all cells which contain a formula. But you are not really interested in the formula, you want to distinguish cells which have a formula from ones which don't. For example, if a cell contains the value 44 (not a formula), then the GET.CELL for that cell would be 44 as would the cell itself. With one caveat which you will see shortly. If it contained =22+22, then the GET.CELL would give "=22+22", but the cell would contain 44. So they'd be unequal. If the GET.CELL is unequal to the cell, then it must contain a formula! So you could try to define a name from cell B1, for example, say "NoFormula" as =GET.CELL(6,'A1'!$E$5)='A1'!$E$5 because if that's TRUE, then there's no formula. To confirm, look at this:

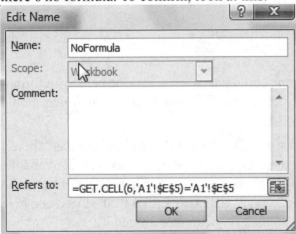

Figure 497

As you can see, it's "False" that it's NoFormula, because it is a formula

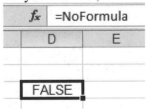

Figure 498

Now change the value in the cell to a number, like 25:

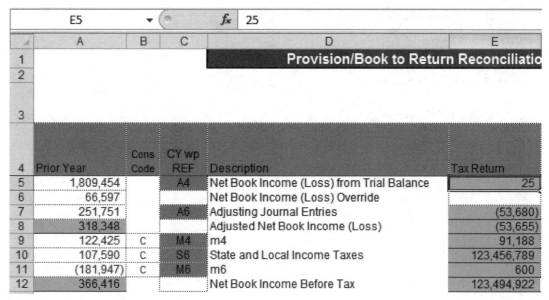

Figure 499

Look at the resulting test:

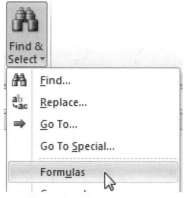

Figure 500

Why is it still False? It should be True! Well, that's because the GET.CELL returns a text value of the cell, and the cell is numeric. That is, 25 is not the same as "25", which is the comparison. So the real answer lies in comparing them both as text, and the new definition of NoFormula should be =GET.CELL(6, 'A1'!E5) &""= 'A1'!E5&"", and it should be relative so you can use it on all cells which should be formulas.

Next step is to use this in conditional formatting on the formulas. So select all the Formula cells:

Figure 501

then apply conditional formatting to them:

Figure 502

Figure 503

and you apply a nice bright yellow to these cells:

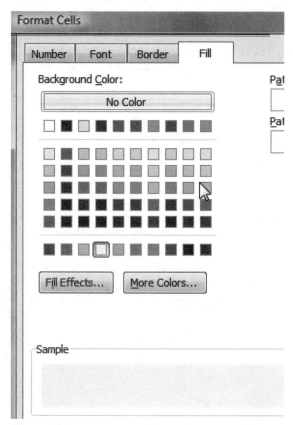

Figure 504

Now look at what happens when you change a value:

	A	B	C	D	E
	E5			f_x 25	
1				Provision/Book to Return Reconcilia	
2					
3					
4	Prior Year	Cons Code	CY wp REF	Description	Tax Return
5	1,809,454		A4	Net Book Income (Loss) from Trial Balance	2
6	66,597			Net Book Income (Loss) Override	
7	251,751		A6	Adjusting Journal Entries	(53,68
8	318,348			Adjusted Net Book Income (Loss)	(53,65
9	122,425	C	M4	m4	91,18
10	107,590	C	S6	State and Local Income Taxes	123,456,78
11	(181,947)	C	M6	m6	60
12	366,416			Net Book Income Before Tax	123,404,09

Figure 505

55-A Piece of Silliness

Question: What's this?

RE1		fx	
	RC	RD	RE	RF
1				
2				
3				
4				
5				
6				
7				
8				
9				
10				
11				
12				
13				
14				
15				
16				
17				
18				
19				
20				
21				
22				

Figure 506

Answer: Calamari! *

Told you it was silly!

*Column RE

INDEX

Also by Bob Umlas

Become an Excel Wizard! Just in time for Excel 2007, This isn't Excel, it's Magic! 2nd edition will save you time and effort. This expanded and enlarged guide is written in a friendly, easy-to-understand style, and is full of screen shots and visuals to help you on your way. ISBN 978-0979215322 .

For people using Excel 2003, the original edition of This isn't Excel, it's Magic contains plenty of amazing tricks from Excel MVP Bob Umlas. ISBN 978-0970827654.

More Books for the Excel Guru